GREAT BASEBALL STORIES

GREAT BASEBALL STORIES

RUMINATIONS AND NOSTALGIC REMINISCENCES ON OUR NATIONAL PASTIME

Edited by Lee Gutkind and Andrew Blauner
Foreword by Yogi Berra

Skyhorse Publishing

Skyhorse Publishing books may be purchased in bulk at special discounts for sales promotion, corporate gifts, fund-raising, or educational purposes. Special editions can also be created to specifications. For details, contact the Special Sales Department, Skyhorse Publishing, 307 West 36th Street, 11th Floor, New York, NY 10018 or info@skyhorsepublishing.com.

Skyhorse® and Skyhorse Publishing® are registered trademarks of Skyhorse Publishing, Inc.®, a Delaware corporation.

Visit our website at www.skyhorsepublishing.com.

10 9 8 7 6 5 4 3 2 1

Library of Congress Cataloging-in-Publication Data is available on file.

ISBN: 978-1-61608-603-9

Printed in China

The editors would like to thank Hattie Fletcher and Donna Hogarty at Creative Nonfiction *for their essential help with coordinating this project. Thanks as well to Keith Gregory, Kathryn Lang, and George Ann Ratchford at Southern Methodist University Press for their friendship and encouragement.*

⚬

The Creative Nonfiction Foundation also thanks the Juliet Lea Hillman Simonds Foundation and the Pennsylvania Council on the Arts, whose generous ongoing support makes all of CNF's projects possible.

CONTENTS

FOREWORD

Yogi Berra

Baseball to me is the greatest game. It's loved and played and watched all over the world. Whenever people ask what I would've done without baseball, I don't know. I played it because it wasn't work, but I worked at it because I loved to play. What I've truly learned is the game is more than a game. Sure it's a business, getting bigger all the time. But it still has an uncanny way of getting into people's hearts and minds—what other business can say that? It's been over a half-century since I last played a major league game, but I observe and follow and read about the game as much as ever. That doesn't mean I'll ever know all there is to know, and that's the beauty. Like I've always said, in baseball you don't know nothing. Or if you ask me a question I don't know, I'm not going to answer. But this much I know. Baseball remains a great game because people still worship and argue about it and they're going to games in record numbers. People still make movies about it. People dream up fantasy teams and go to fantasy camps. People keep analyzing and concocting statistics. And authors never stop writing about the game. Simply, baseball makes great baseball literature. The tittle of the previous edition of this book is no medical book—if it was, I'm certain I wouldn't have read it. It's a baseball book, and a good one, and it's nice to be in a lineup that includes some pretty good writers. A good book makes you think about things you might not already think about. Or enjoy stories from writers you maybe don't know. Of course, I was never good with writers' names. A long time ago, somebody introduced me to Ernest Hemingway, mentioning that he was a great writer. So I asked, "Which paper?" That was when most of my reading consisted of the sports pages and comic books. But Hemingway was a big baseball fan. No surprise he used the game in his writing, especially in *The Old Man and the Sea*, referring to my old teammate Joe DiMaggio and the main character missing the daily box scores. Baseball has its own literature. It even has its own language. The game goes back to before the Civil War, but it never gets old. Neither does a good baseball book.

—September 2007

INTRODUCTION
BASEBALL: THE UNIVERSAL CONNECTION

Lee Gutkind

During the spring of 2007, I taught a graduate-level writing workshop in creative nonfiction to a group of students, mostly fiction writers, enrolled in the MFA program at Arizona State University, where I was serving as writer-in-residence. When I teach this type of course, I usually assign at least one immersion essay; I choose a general subject and ask my students to involve themselves in it somehow and write about what they learn and experience.

There are several reasons for this immersion assignment. I want emerging creative nonfiction writers to understand that there are often subjects more important and more interesting than themselves; that there's a rich and colorful world, with an unlimited cast of characters, just waiting to be captured dramatically in prose, wherever you live or visit; and that writers, especially students, need to try to remove themselves from their campuses and neighborhoods and experience new things.

I also want students to see how many different angles there are to any given subject. There are unlimited potential crevices and corners to mine for essay material—enough for each member of a class to choose a different approach. I have used medicine and dogs as subject prompts in Pittsburgh, where I usually teach, and bullfighting in Spain. At Arizona State, I chose baseball, because almost half of major league baseball teams conduct spring training nearby; there are at least four ballparks within a half-hour drive of Tempe, near Phoenix, where ASU is located, and two in walking distance—depending, of course, on the heat of the day.

I have to admit that immersion is not a universally popular assignment. For one thing, it forces more work on students than writing straight memoir; they must research a subject, something they don't know a lot about, and take the time—day or night, holiday and weekend, on a somewhat regular basis—to meet the right people and find a story worth telling.

Although I cannot say my students were chomping at the bit to go to the ballpark, I did immediately notice the way in which baseball (the subject, if not the assignment) brought them together. There were three men in the class—Jake, Aaron, and Cameron—and although they had grown up in different parts of the country, discussions of baseball made their differences in background seem almost nonexistent. They shared a common language, from discussing ballparks in their hometowns and comparing them with parks they had visited in Arizona and elsewhere, to the ways in which their favorite players held their bats, along with baseball memories and legacies passed on to them by their fathers and mentors.

I would often sit in class and listen to their conversations and hear the familiar echoes of my own past conversations with friends many years ago, and although the names were different, the subject matter, the observations, and in-jokes were pretty much the same. I remember thinking how marvelous it was, this connective tissue between the generations.

As it happens, each of the men in my class actually played baseball in some sort of organized fashion, whether in Little League or high school. And one of the things that sets baseball apart from other popular sports, say, football or basketball, is its accessibility to players—it's still a sport many boys grow up playing. Perhaps this accounts for the deep inside knowledge many of the writers in *Great Baseball Stories* display for various aspects of the game. Matt Wood, who knows from experience, writes about the challenges and joys of playing first base. George Plimpton writes about the indignity of being demoted from pitcher to first baseman to rightfielder, but finds the space to think great thoughts in the outfield, as does J. D. Scrimgeour, whose outfield is more a state of mind than a geographic location.

Other writers chose to focus on equipment. The paraphernalia of baseball represent a significant level of personal connection and intimacy shared by few other sports. In "The Bat," Philip Deaver recalls a time when "an eleven-year-old . . . could eye the ash or hickory and see promise in the grain of the wood, tell what felt right in the distribution of the weight between the handle and the barrel." The strongest connection in baseball, however, may be the one between player and glove, which is perhaps why there are three essays here focusing on the beloved "mitt." The glove, of course, touches the player, connects him to the game, and protects him from harm. But the connection between player and glove extends beyond the physical: "To play baseball well," Stefan Fatsis writes in his biography of his glove, "you have to consider your glove an ideal; if not, it will let you down."

Interestingly, one of the pieces about gloves in this collection was written by a woman, Katherine Powers (the third is by Christopher Buckley), whose connection to her glove is as strong as any man's, although she never played baseball in an organized fashion and the story of her glove is in many ways the story of her attempt to find people with whom to play ball. What I found with the assignment I gave my class—which included a half dozen women—was that although the women did not share the same level of personal experience with the game as players, nevertheless through their fathers, brothers, boyfriends, and teachers they had strong personal connections to the sport that they could draw on.

Although the clear majority of essays in this collection were written by men, the four essays written by women tell stories about the significance of baseball in the writers' lives and reflect on the authors' connections to the sport as women and as individuals. Susan Perabo writes about her fantasy career and assesses the likelihood that women will ever play in the major leagues; Elizabeth Bobrick remembers several years when being an avid fan of the Baltimore Orioles helped her realize her own strength; and Caitlin Horrocks writes about how playing a Finnish variation of baseball—and being good at it—helped her finally become "the grateful citizen of a baseball nation."

Of course, as Frank Deford points out in his whimsical "An Ode to Baseball Caps," we are all—players and nonplayers, fans and nonfans—citizens of a baseball nation, one in which "baseball caps are now bigger than baseball . . . [and] may well even be the most familiar American artifact, passing Coca-Cola and blue jeans and bad movies."

Baseball, of course, is commonly held to reflect some essential part of the American spirit, a phenomenon demonstrated vividly in expatriate Rick Harsch's essay about managing a team in Slovenia. Kevin Baker tells the story of the early ballparks and argues that baseball—contrary to the myth about it being first played in Abner Doubleday's meadow in Cooperstown—has always been a city game, and uniquely American. "Just as the country seemed to stretch away forever before the first immigrants, so the ball field is theoretically infinite," he writes. What's more, "it was in the new ballparks . . . that a true assimilation of American men of all classes would actually take place, and usually on a much closer and more intimate basis than ever occurred in other public parks."

Although baseball is no longer the only game in town and arguably occupies a somewhat diminished role in American culture, still it holds the promise of bringing families and communities together. In "Take Me Back to the Ball Game," Warren Goldstein recounts his family's attempt to find common ground on the field one summer. In "The Southworths," set against the backdrop of World War II, Michael Shapiro tells the story of a manager father and pilot son whose correspondence centered around the father's team's wins and losses. Jeff Greenfield discusses the ways in which trips to Yankee Stadium have created memories across three generations of his family.

And as fans, we often find an extended family in the stands among strangers. In "Ya Gotta Believe," John Thorn traces the etymology of fandom and provides a psychological assessment of the typical fan ("Baseball in America is a sort of faith for the faithless," he writes), and in "Freddy the Fan," Sean Wilentz introduces readers to one vociferous and memorable Yankee fan and imagines possible exhibits for a Baseball Fans' Hall of Fame.

No doubt, the sport attracts passionate followers. In "Spring Training Lights," Jake Young tells the story of how the light poles from the Polo Grounds, home to the New York Giants, ended up in the Arizona desert watching over spring training games played by the Oakland Athletics. During his research, Young spends time in online communities devoted to debating the finer points of ballpark history—for example, whether during the 1962 renovation at the Polo Grounds the grandstands were painted green, blue, or a "color which is a more bluish-green, but still more green than blue."

Young, incidentally, was a student in my Arizona workshop, as was Caitlin Horrocks. It is rare that I publish my students' work (while they are my students), but

Caitlin and Jake are exceptional writers, and their essays are fine examples of immersion reporting as well as fascinating stories about unexpected and specific aspects of baseball.

Ultimately, the common allure of baseball helped the members of my class come together—and it's what brings this collection together. There is something irresistible about the sport that reaches across generations and through time, regardless of nationality or geography.

I should say that love and respect for baseball also brought together the makers of this collection. Keith Gregory, director of Southern Methodist University Press, is an avid fan, while Andrew Blauner, my coeditor, a well-respected literary agent in New York—he represents me and *Creative Nonfiction*—also has a long history with the sport, not only as a former high school player but as a fan, as he puts it, "at Yankee Stadium, Cape Cod League, or a pickup game in a playground anywhere." Andrew is, as well, a connoisseur of sports writing; he is the editor of a well-received collection of essays encompassing baseball and other sports, called *Coach: Writers Reflect on People Who Made a Difference,* and his connections and insights were tremendously helpful in bringing this collection together.

It is rare that agents and writers work together in the way in which Andrew and I have worked on *Great Baseball Stories.* I like to think our working relationship is rooted in mutual appreciation of literature and an appreciation for the challenges and rewards of narrative nonfiction writing. Our strong relationship, as represented in this collection, also has to do with the connective tissue of the game of baseball itself, which is essential and perhaps—as American culture becomes universalized and baseball players, like other superstars, are seduced by money and media—endangered. The essays in *Great Baseball Stories* isolate essential aspects of the game—equipment, field positions, the fields themselves—but what ties them together is our common nostalgia for the way it was, and our fervent hope that the sport will endure the way we think it always should be.

GREAT BASEBALL STORIES

AT THE PARK

Kevin Baker

Baseball to me is an addiction, and as such, a distraction from writing—but some distractions are badly needed. What I love about baseball is that it doesn't have any greater meaning; it's just a beautiful thing in its own right. I love its rituals, its carefully cultivated history. I love the fact that it's a link to the American past, especially in its peculiarities. Hence my love of old ballparks: they were eccentric without trying to be so, which is appealing in our very purposeful, homogenized time. Even the attempts to consciously re-create them, worthy though they are, don't quite work. The past is quite dead, and well beyond us, which gives it its luster.

> *Some boy too far from town to learn baseball, Whose only play was what he found himself . . .*

—Robert Frost, "Birches"

I t always was a city game, baseball.

That's not how the old pastoralists would have it, of course. They have so loaded the game down with country imagery that it's hard to separate the mythology from the reality now—little boys chasing fly balls into Iowa cornfields, The Natural peeling a bat off a lightning-damned tree. When it came time to build a Hall of Fame the lords of the game stuck it up in bucolic Cooperstown, seizing upon some old-timer's letter about how the game was invented in Abner Doubleday's meadow.

Doubleday was the Forrest Gump of the nineteenth century, a Union officer who was there at Fort Sumter, there at Gettysburg. But he wasn't even around for the invention of baseball.

The game required too many boys, as Frost's words imply. Only those who have forgotten the punishing isolation of American rural life would believe baseball came of age in the country. The old names give it away. It was called "town ball," because it was played on those days when everybody came into town for church, or market. It was called "the New York game," because that's where baseball—real baseball—actually started, in vacant lots around what is now the West Side Manhattan neighborhood of Chelsea. It was played not by country boys but by clubs of middle-class merchants with a little leisure time on their hands; then increasingly by sharp-eyed immigrant professionals, Pat and Mick and Heinie.

The first major-league parks, back in the nineteenth century, were little more than sandlots with rows of precarious wooden bleachers—one step up from those vacant, rock-strewn lots in Chelsea. Eventually they were ringed, frontier-style, with a stockade fence so the owners could monopolize what was going on inside—charge for admission and food sales; shake down or expel gamblers who dogged the game; expand the fan base to the growing middle class, to children, and even women. These changes were akin to Vegas going family—or to the incandescent cities of fire that rose along the sands of Coney Island during the same period, replacing the site of louche entertainments with the very first official amusement parks.

The crowds often broke the walls on the afternoons of big games. But like the cities in which they were contained, the parks were steadily improved by fire. Just as the city's wood shanties were replaced by ornate, block-long apartment buildings, by skyscrapers and bridges, and grand railroad stations and gorgeous, humming, electrical generators, the ballparks were replaced by concrete-and-steel structures that sprouted second tiers and outfield bleachers—everything getting bigger and better, all the time.

Just as the country seemed to stretch away forever before the first immigrants, so the ball field is theoretically infinite, the foul lines moving ever farther away from each other until they encompass all of existence. How to traverse this infinite landscape? Just as American industrialists, confronted with seemingly boundless plenty, invented time management, trying to convert all they saw before them into a rational system of production, so, too, have baseball's acolytes always tried to break the game down into more and more precise statistics, some narrative that will allow us to measure every movement on the field.

⬤ ⬤ ⬤

Air, space, and recreation were the crying needs of the American city by the mid-nineteenth century. They were considered vital to the continued health of both the individual and the polis. No city had a public park of any size. Those wishing relief from the city's racket and bustle resorted to the new rural cemeteries. These had begun to spring up with the consecration of Cambridge's Mount Auburn Cemetery in 1831, followed by Philadelphia's Laurel Hill (1836), and Brooklyn's vast Green-Wood Cemetery (1838). These were full-scale necropolises, laid out in the British landscaping style of improved nature, with deliberately winding roads, and strategically placed trees, bushes, ponds, hillocks, and even boulders, designed to maximize dramatic views and uplifting vistas. The need for such spaces was quickly evidenced by their immense popularity. City dwellers poured out to the new cemeteries for Sunday afternoon picnics, whether a loved one was buried there or not. Green-Wood, by far the most splendid and the largest of the scenic graveyards at 478 acres, was drawing sixty thousand visitors a year soon after it opened for business.

"Rural cemeteries provided fresh air and greenery—and the illusion of a beautiful countryside," points out Frederick Law Olmsted biographer Witold Rybczynski.

Yet cemeteries were inherently limited by their utility, and there were still fears about the unhealthful "miasmas" that reputedly leaked up from the graves. Soon, Olmsted and his longtime partner Calvert Vaux had begun to lay out one magnificent public park after another in cities across the United States. These were deliberately intended as places of moral improvement as well as physical and cultural relief. Clean air and a place to stretch the legs were just the start. A dairy was actually built in New York's Central Park, intended to provide free, wholesome milk for the city's poor at a time when it was in short supply. Museums, concert halls, and other cultural institutions were to dot the park's perimeters. Beyond this, the poor were to benefit simply by exposure to their betters.

"There need to be places and times for re-unions [where] the rich and poor, the cultivated and the self-made, shall be attracted together and encouraged to assimilate," Olmsted wrote.

Baseball, on the other hand, wasn't thought to improve anybody. The game itself was all but banned from Central Park for decades. Yet it was in the new ballparks—the only other large open spaces in most American cities, coming into their own just as the first wave of public park building was coming to an end—that a true assimilation of American men of all classes would actually take place, and usually on a much closer and more intimate basis than ever occurred in other public parks.

The new ballparks were gloriously eccentric. For all of their corporate purpose, there was a specificity to them, an endearing individuality that would all but vanish from American business life. No other sport would ever boast such idiosyncratic playing fields. And in no other sport would the field become so critical to how the game itself was played, or such an enduring part of its lore.

Unlike the cemeteries and the English-style woods, or even the raucous amuse-

ment parks, the ballparks remained quintessentially urban structures. They were wedged into street lots, built around railroads and streetcar lines, factories and breweries and livery stables, rivers and highways, and the topography surrounding the parks gave rise to the quirks in their design. Brooklyn's Dodgers got their name because players and spectators alike had to dodge the trolleys to get to their old Washington Park field. Washington's Griffith Stadium featured a right angle in dead centerfield, a bulge where five homeowners had refused to sell. Cincinnati's Crosley Field shot some 377 feet out to rightfield, but was only 328 feet to leftfield, in which there was also a small hillock that sent Babe Ruth sprawling in the last year of his career. The Dodgers' later home at Ebbets Field featured a 20-foot-high chain-link fence in rightfield above a concave wall and a scoreboard with its immortal lower panel advertising borough president Abe Stark's clothing store at 1514 Pitkin Avenue: "Hit Sign, Win Suit."

Every stadium had its own peculiarities. The ones we know best are the thick ivy that clings to the lovely brick walls of Chicago's Wrigley Field and the great green wall looming over left in Boston's Fenway Park, but this is just because these are the only two major-league parks to have survived from the era before World War I. So many of the others, now vanished, had their own gratuitous grace notes. As early as 1902, Cincinnati had built the short-lived Palace of the Fans, complete with grand Beaux Arts columns and pillars modeled after the White City at the 1893 Columbian Exposition in Chicago—the source of the City Beautiful movement in America. The new Polo Grounds was festooned with coats-of-arms, representing all the National League clubs, along the top of the grandstand. The top of the original Yankee Stadium's upper deck dripped with white filigree bunting, and monuments to beloved former players and managers were actually installed on the playing field. Philadelphia's Shibe Park had a conical, domed tower, an escaped turret from some upper-middle-class apartment house, over its main entrance. There was the Jury Box in Boston's Braves Field bleachers; the Coop, and the Crow's Nest, and the open-air promenade at Pittsburgh's Forbes Field. Ebbets Field had an 80-foot Italian-marble floor in the image of a baseball in its rotunda, and a 27-foot-high domed ceiling, from which hung a chandelier with twelve baseball-bat arms that held globes of lights shaped like baseballs.

The ticket windows at the old-time parks tended to look like boathouses or beach pavilions, with fringed awnings and gentle arches. At Ebbets, they were gilded. The grandstands were always steep and close, dark and mysterious in their back rows after night baseball was instituted. Just beyond the walls of each park were comforting, orienting urban features of one sort or another: the Bronx County Courthouse, the flashing Citgo sign over Kenmore, the gloomy Cathedral of Learning towering over the leftfield wall in Pittsburgh, clouds of locomotive smoke billowing up from the Boston and Albany tracks behind left and center in Braves Field. There were usually, as well, huge, hand-operated scoreboards somewhere out in centerfield, visible to all. They showed the line scores of the same sixteen teams in the same eleven cities for fifty years, time moving on in the same stately progression, inning by inning.

The one feature all the old ballparks shared was outfields that were prodigious by today's standards. The old parks were routinely 420 feet to the farthest reaches of centerfield, and often 360–375 feet down the lines. It was 462 feet to center at Forbes Field, and 461 to left-center in Yankee Stadium. The Yankees' previous home, Hilltop Park, stretched an endless 542 feet across the rough sod of Washington Heights. There were practical reasons for this. In the dead ball era, much of the scoring came from balls that found a seam and just kept on rolling. For an important game, the overflow crowd might be put out behind a rope in the outfield, and perhaps their cars or buggies, too.

• • •

The most fantastic ballpark of all was the Polo Grounds, the home of the New York Giants, in upper Harlem. It was a strange place, and strange things happened there. The only man ever killed on a major-league playing field, Ray Chapman, died at home plate, hit in the head by a pitch. A fan once died in the stands there, too, between games of a doubleheader, struck by a stray bullet fired from a neighborhood rooftop. He went so quietly that no one realized he was dead at first; they thought he was only nodding off in the grandstand on a sunny summer afternoon.

No one ever played polo there; the name was carried over from the Giants' previous digs, James Bennett's old polo field down at 110th Street and Fifth Avenue. The new park the team built for itself in 1889 at 156th–157th Streets and Eighth Avenue was shaped like a gigantic horseshoe facing the Harlem River—the last major-league ballpark that ever did or probably ever will disrupt the crowded streets of Manhattan Island. (In fact, as late as 1874, the whole site was *under* the Harlem River.)

Down the lines were the easiest home run shots in the big leagues, 279 feet to left and 257 to right. In some clairvoyant presentiment of Frank Gehry's undulating architecture, the outfield walls stretched all the way out to a centerfield 483 feet from home plate. There, filling the gap in the horseshoe, were a multistory set of clubhouses and team offices, with a monument at the field level to Eddie Grant, a former Giants player killed in World War I; a large, square Longines clock crowning the top of the building; and a huge cigarette ad—"Always Buy Chesterfields"—in between. Two sets of stairs led to the field from the clubhouses, so that the players from both teams had to enter and exit the field matador-like, accepting the ovations and the jeers and barbs of the fans all around them.

It was the most glamorous park of the dead ball era, when the close, fast game was played mostly inside the infield, and always in the afternoon. John "Muggsy" McGraw, the irascible manager and part-owner of the Giants, would invite his show business celebrities up in the afternoon. They could park their beautiful new auto-mobiles—as varied and idiosyncratic as the ballparks themselves—on the edge of the outfield and take in a whole nine innings before motoring back down to Broad-way in time for the evening curtain. McGraw, "the Little Napoleon," did what he wanted: consorted with gamblers, owned part of a pool hall, punched umpires, and feuded with league presidents. It was a pitcher's game, and McGraw had the great-est one alive, his close friend and housemate, Christy Mathewson, the all-American boy grown up. A college man, Matty was as handsome and tall and well-spoken as McGraw was short and profane and dumpy; he had an easy grace about him and an out pitch known by the lovely old-fashioned name of "fadeaway."

Then everything changed, practically right before McGraw's eyes. The gamblers who hung out at McGraw's own favorite off-field stomping grounds, Manhattan's Ansonia Hotel—a confection no less unlikely in history or appearance than the Polo Grounds, the building where Bette Midler would get her start in a gay bathhouse, and Plato's Retreat would have its brief, notorious reign (but that's another story)—

The Polo Grounds 1923. *Photo Courtesy of Library of Congress, George Bain Collection.*

were busy plotting the fix that would throw the 1919 World Series. A hero was needed, and he would appear in the most unlikely dugout.

The Yankees were the Giants' tenants, their poor relations in the Polo Grounds, when they acquired Babe Ruth from the Red Sox. No deal ever irked Muggsy more. He hated Ruth, right from the beginning, with his seemingly heedless style of play and his ability to hog the spotlight. Most unforgivably, Ruth would transform the game, take it away forever from the control of the manager with his canny, small-ball strategies.

Matty went off to fight World War I and returned a dying man, his lungs burned out in a training accident. Meanwhile, the Babe lofted one pop fly after another down the short foul lines of the Polo Grounds and launched moonshots all the way out to the distant bleachers. He had, somehow, transcended the old geometry of the game. It was all about power now. The infinite spaces of the old ball field had suddenly been spanned. The distant fans intimately connected with their hero as they scrambled for the balls he dropped in their midst, and roared their tribute during his leisurely, majestic strolls around the bases. The infinite spaces of the Polo Grounds—of *baseball*—had suddenly been negated.

McGraw hated it. So did all the old baseball purists. In every sport there are those—usually sportswriters—who remain irrevocably opposed to spectacular, flashy play. These individuals, who can be found on your sports page to this day, have yet to accept the home run in baseball, the forward pass in football, the long jump shot in basketball—even seventy, eighty, ninety years after these innovations came to pass. To purists, such plays make the game look too easy, almost cheap. They seem to negate the hard work and on-field canniness that defined the old Baltimore Oriole teams McGraw had cut his teeth on back in the nineteenth century.

• • •

Ruth was altogether *too much*, the consummate player of the 1920s. He himself had made the crossing from the old game to the new, the best southpaw in the now-dead dead ball game, before effortlessly converting himself into a slugger—the first true slugger anyone had ever seen. Before him, home runs were as likely to be inside-the-park jobs as they were to land in the stands. The leading power hitters rarely hit more than 12 or 15 in a season; the entire Yankees *team* hit all of 8 in 1913, their first year in John McGraw's park. But here was Ruth now, setting new records for home runs nearly every season—29, 54, 59 . . . eventually 60 in 1927, or more than any other whole team in the American League hit that year. The suddenly rich, star-laden Yankees shook the dust of the Polo Grounds from their feet at McGraw's insistence, but the manager couldn't turn back time by banishing the team to the outer boroughs. The Yankees moved into their own stadium, "The House That Ruth Built," in the toney new Bronx, and won pennant after pennant, setting new attendance records.

We know Ruth today mostly from a handful of salvaged photographs and film clips. He seems like a caricature now, a joke, with that big, puffy, tragicomic clown's face. A grainy figure with an enormous pot belly, flicking at the ball with his bat and then skittering around the bases on his spindly legs, smiling and nodding, smiling and tipping his cap. We have heard all the stories about his gargantuan appetites, about all the endless hot dogs, the oceans of booze, Ty Cobb seeing him in a whorehouse the night before a game with three—or was it four?—women, a tray of beer, and another one of pig knuckles . . . then watching him hit two home runs the next day, waddling around the bases complaining about how his stomach hurt.

That Babe surely existed, as did the Babe who seems to have actually put himself on the disabled list through overeating and the Babe who signed baseballs for sick boys in hospital beds and told them he was going to hit home runs for them. But there was another Babe, too, an earlier Babe we don't like to dwell on so much because he reveals another side of the game. This was the young Babe, before he had grown the great gut, an athlete of phenomenal, almost frightening quickness and skill. To watch him in action, barreling around the bases, running through anything that gets in his way, is like watching a force of nature. In photographs his eyes flash under his dark brow, not yet safely encased in flesh. It is the look that suggests other appetites besides the culinary. It is the face of another street kid, with an eye out for his opportunities in the big city.

Contrary to Muggsy's assumptions, this Ruth was not inattentive to his game, but had an innate, fundamental feel for the sport. This was the Babe who stole home seventeen times, who was an excellent bunter, hit to the opposite field, had a mean hook slide. The Babe who was an outstanding outfielder, who before games would sometimes give the fans a thrill by laying a towel down on home plate and seeing how many times he could hit it on the fly from deep rightfield. When he was in a slump at the plate, he might break out of it by pitching batting practice, or even catching a few pitches, trying to get his timing back.

Mobbed wherever he went, Ruth rarely lost his geniality, and then usually only when sorely provoked. He moved amiably through life, always smiling and winking, calling all the strangers who pursued him "kid." He took the vicious bench-jockeying of the era in stride and delighted in returning it.

The only taunt that ever got to him was when someone called him *nigger*. It infuriated him, which only made rumors persist. *Could* he have been? It is a repugnant question, of course, even if one might wish it were so—even if it would be the best possible joke on organized white baseball, which thought it had banned all African Americans from its midst. It is not worth the query, though; it is unknowable. Suffice it to say that Ruth was another mongrel American city boy like most of us—like all the rest of us, whether we want to admit it or not. The son of a Baltimore barkeep and his wife, he was handed over to a Catholic orphanage at a young age. The Jesuit fathers set him free in 1914—the same year Louis Armstrong was turned loose from the New Orleans boys' home he had been confined to for a youthful indiscretion. Two teenaged boys, released from two Southern homes, each about to transform his own piece of popular culture forever—such was the energy of America at the time.

The ban on black ballplayers—*known* black players—in the major leagues finally ended in 1947, with Jackie Robinson. Within four years, a final legend would be playing in the Polo Grounds. Willie Mays was in many ways the antithesis of Ruth. Shorter and more slender at five-eleven, 180 pounds, Mays was all elegance and fluidity, a player whose grace caused grown men to mourn his passing from New York for decades. If the Babe had been singular in conquering the two great poles of the game, pitching and hitting, it is doubtful there ever was as complete an all-around player as Willie Mays—a five-skill player, as the terminology has it. He could hit, hit for power, field, throw, run—how he could run. He ran out from under his hat, he was so fast. He was the first man in over 30 years to hit over 30 home runs and steal over 30 bases in the same season. He hit over 50 home runs on two separate occasions, once into the wind off San Francisco Bay.

He could do anything—gliding through life, it seemed, even more smoothly than Ruth had. Greeting all the adoring strangers with his own generic salute, "*Say hey!*" A good-natured if somewhat removed young man, up from Birmingham; up from nowhere, coached mainly by his father, a former Negro League star. Bursting on the scene a fully formed major-leaguer, it seemed. Bursting out with all that incalculable, bottled-up talent, that angry, channeled intensity those first, remarkable generations of no-longer banned black players brought to the big leagues—Robinson and Mays, and Newcombe and Frank Robinson and Aaron and Gibson and Clemente, to name just a few. Though Mays never seemed that angry. Enjoying himself, like Ruth. Even playing stickball out on the streets of Harlem with the neighborhood kids, waving a broomstick bat at the spaldeen, splattering it over the manhole covers.

September 29, 1954: the first game of the World Series at the Polo Grounds. The strange old park has less than ten years to live, and Mays, twenty-three, in his first full major-league season, is about to impress his image indelibly on the history of the game—and to ensure that a last glimpse of the old ballpark will be preserved in countless highlight reels. It's the eighth inning of a tie game, two on and nobody out for the visiting Cleveland Indians, and Vic Wertz, a muscular first baseman, is at the plate. Wertz will be red-hot throughout the Series, and he has already recorded three hits on the day, a triple and two singles. Now he rips another soaring fly, deep into the endless expanses of the Polo Grounds' right-centerfield.

Mays is after the ball. It keeps going, and he is right after it. Running and running, *outrunning* the ball, miraculously bisecting the endless expanses of the ball field, running all the way out over the vast, dark fields of the republic. Here is the weird centerfield clubhouse coming into view now, the monument to Eddie Grant, killed in the Great War, the war that took poor Matty's lungs. Here is a strange scene, frozen in still unfinished reaction: a few faces, peering out of the clubhouse windows, unable to see just where Mays is; a few of the fans, most of them men wearing hats, and some in jackets, too, even in the centerfield bleachers, just beginning to stand up, just aware something is going on that doesn't add up. They are all captured forever, in this first twitch of a great realization.

For Mays has already caught the ball. Running straight out, he has caught it over his left shoulder with barely a shrug. He is already turning back to the infield and about to throw, even as the crowd is still beginning to bestir itself. He windmills a quick throw back toward the plate, and the runners are kept from scoring. The Giants get out of the inning, win the game, sweep the World Series—the only one Mays will win in his whole long incomparable career.

It was the greatest catch ever made in the World Series, perhaps the greatest catch ever. Bob Feller, the great Cleveland pitcher watching from the dugout that day, sniffed later that no one thought it was the greatest catch *then*. Feller, unaccountably sour for a man blessed with a hundred mile-an-hour fastball, claimed that everyone *knew* Mays used to deliberately wear his hats too small so they would fall off and make everything he did look faster, better, more incredible.

But the pictures of that frozen moment show that Mays's hat is just falling off *then*, obviously jarred off by how suddenly he has stopped and turned to make the throw. In fairness, it is easy to see how Feller or any other onlooker could be deceived. The over-the-shoulder catch is the hardest single play in baseball, but watching the film to this day, a casual observer will not see anything very dramatic, will notice little that stands out from the fantastic fluidity of Mays in motion. The greatness of the catch lies in how effortless Mays has made it look—lies in *where* he is, how far he has had to travel just to *be* there. He has bridged the same gap as Ruth did with his moonshots, but he has done it as a single running man catching up to the slugger's ball, closing the circle.

More than a decade later, they were still selling boys' models of Mays running down Wertz's ball—preserving at least some little, plastic representation of the old Polo Grounds. Mays would leave when Horace Stoneham, the Giants' drunk of an owner, was lured out to the West Coast, abandoning the stickball-playing kids on the streets of Harlem without a second glance. The Polo Grounds was torn down in 1964, replaced by an ill-considered housing project. Nearly all of the old ballparks met a similar fate over the next few decades—Ebbets Field and Shibe Park, Forbes Field and Crosley Field, Sportsman's Park and Comiskey Park, and Tiger Stadium—as the club owners squirmed and ran to get away from anyplace there might be black people; to where they could find something much more vital, which is to say, parking. The old parks would be replaced, at first, by new stadiums mostly out in the suburbs—round, interchangeable, all-purpose stadiums, many carpeted with artificial turf, that could be used just as easily for football games or rock concerts.

The Mets brought Mays back to play in what may have been the ugliest of them all, Shea Stadium, a park that already looked irredeemably shabby when it was brand-new. He was forty-two years old when he appeared in the 1973 World Series, and even though he managed to drive in the winning run in one game off a future Hall of Fame pitcher, he staggered sadly about the outfield, misplaying balls. Everyone gasped that Willie Mays had grown old, and in his embarrassment he retired after that fall.

He had lasted, in the end, nearly as long as the terrible new cookie-cutter ballparks would. Trying to capitalize on memories and luxury boxes, the owners found an excuse to tear down most of them after only a generation or so. In one town after another, baseball has returned to the inner cities, to new parks that were ostentatiously designed with quirky, eccentric features—a rightfield wall that is part of an old warehouse, a small knoll in deep center, even a swimming pool in the bleachers. They are improvements over the round, bleak stadiums of the 1960s—though somehow they never recaptured the beauty of the old parks, revealing themselves, ultimately, as what they were: an exercise in ready-made nostalgia. The past, once uncoupled, is not so easily regained.

Kevin Baker is the author of four novels, including the City of Fire trilogy: *Dreamland, Paradise Alley,* and *Strivers Row.* He is currently at work on a nonfiction book about the history of New York City baseball.

MY GLOVE: A BIOGRAPHY

Stefan Fatsis

When I was asked to contribute to this anthology about the gorgeous minutiae of baseball, I didn't have to think for even a second about a topic. I'd wanted to write about my baseball glove for years. Not only is it the single most personal object I own—the one thing I would be devastated to lose—it is my last, best connection to the baseball that defined my life as a kid. Not just playing the game incessantly, but being a crazy fan of it, too. My glove is a reminder that the innocence and thrill that made baseball so great and so important still exist in this thirty-year-old hunk of leather.

"**I**'ll tell you what. It's sure broken in perfect."

In my forty-three years on Earth, this ranks among the highest compliments I have received. Right up there, definitely top five, maybe No. 1. So tell me more, Bob Clevenhagen, you curmudgeonly craftsman extraordinaire, you seen-it-all, stitched-'em-all Boswell of the baseball glove, you National Archive of five-fingered-leather historical facts and figures, you Ravel of Rawlings Sporting Goods.

"It's broken in as well as any I ever get," Bob says. On the other end of the telephone line, I smile so hard that blood vessels threaten to pop in my cheeks. After all, Bob has been making and repairing gloves for current and future Hall of Famers for three decades. "The target for you is the base of your index finger, not the web. That's the way the pro player would do it. Not the retail market. Not a softball player."

Hell, no! Not the retail market! Not a softball player!

"This looks like a major-league gamer."

I move from happiness to rapture. In fact, I might just cry.

"That's high praise," I manage to say, filling dead air when what I really want to do is drop the phone and dance.

"Yes, it is," Bob replies, curt, gruff, no nonsense, Midwestern. He's just the third person in the 119-year history of Rawlings to hold the exalted title of Glove Designer, not a man given to bromides and bon mots, which of course makes his words all the sweeter. "Yours looks like—well, look in the Hall of Fame."

I may spontaneously combust.

"Those gloves probably look just like yours. Same color, same shape, same faded-out look," he says. "It's just a nice-looking glove."

● ● ●

My glove isn't just broken in perfect, to quote Bob. I believe it is stunningly perfect, consummately perfect, why-would-anyone-use-anything-else? perfect. To play baseball well, you have to consider your glove an ideal; if not, it will let you down. A glove has to feel like an extension of your hand, something over which you have the motor control of a surgeon repairing a capillary. But my glove is more than just a piece of equipment that works for me. I really think it is empirically flawless.

Let's start with its shape: parabolic from the top of the thumb to the tip of the pinkie. This is the result of years of pushing those two fingers toward the middle; there's a slight break about three inches from the end of each digit. No ball is leaving my glove because it bent back one of the outermost fingers.

When I put the glove on, the first thing I inevitably do is press down the index finger. This transforms the parabola into a circle. Open your palm and spread your fingers wide. Now curl your fingertips forward. That's what my stationary glove looks like.

My glove is soft. It collapses of its own accord when set down. But, thanks to its aforementioned shape, it never falls completely flat, full thumb atop full pinkie. Instead, the tip of the thumb and the tip of the pinkie touch delicately, like God reaching out to Adam on the ceiling of the Sistine Chapel. I've never understood gloves that open to a V and shut like a book. The idea is to catch a round ball, not a triangular block. Roundness is essential. Softness is, too. The trick is to create a glove pliable enough to respond to your slightest movement. To bend to a player's will, a glove needs to bend. Mine does.

The index finger of my left hand—I throw righthanded—lies on the exterior of the glove's back, the only digit not tucked inside. This technique provides bonus protection when catching hard-hit or fast-thrown balls. I believe it also helps me better control the glove's behavior. And it looks cool.

Each finger curves gently, like a suburban cul-de-sac. The adjustable loops surrounding the pinkie and thumb aren't tied too tightly, but their existence is palpable. The web isn't soft and deep, so that a ball might get lost, but rather follows the natural curvature from the top of the index finger to the top of the thumb. The heel of my glove aligns with the heel of my palm. The shearling beneath the wrist strap is matted but still recognizable. There are no garish personal adornments, just my first initial and last name written meticulously in black ink letters three-eighths of an inch tall just above the seam along the thumb. It looks as if I used a ruler to line the letters up.

Then there's the smell: leather, dirt, grass, saliva, sun, spring, childhood, summer, hope, skill, anticipation, achievement, fulfillment, memory, love, joy.

● ● ●

I bought my glove in the spring of 1977. I was about to turn fourteen, out of Little League and over my head in the ninety-feet-to-first-base Senior League in the inner suburb of Pelham, New York. A wall of leather graced the sporting goods store in a nearby town, soft porn in my baseball-centric world. I had to have a Rawlings—it would be my third or fourth Rawlings, one of them royal blue—because that's what major leaguers wore. And it had to be a good one because, while every other kid pined for his turn at bat, I happily chased grounders until dark. Five feet tall and under a hundred pounds, I was a typical prepubescent second baseman: all field, no hit. An adult-sized glove would make me feel bigger, and play bigger.

My choice, the XPG6, was expensive. I remember the price as ninety dollars, though old Rawlings catalogues tell me it was probably seventy dollars (or we were ripped off). I didn't know it then, but it was fourth-priciest glove in the Rawlings line. Thanks, Mom, for not blinking.

Not insignificantly, the XPG6 reminded me of the glove my eight-years older brother wore when he was in high school. Virtually all of my decisions at that age were influenced by my brother, who had taught me how to calculate my batting average when I was in the second grade. (At age nine, clearly my athletic prime, I hit .750, aided, no doubt, by some generous scoring.) He played shortstop and, like me, was a competent but unexceptional player. But his glove was just right: round and bendable. I didn't want his, just one like it.

So the XPG6 it was. It bore Rawlings's famous trademarks: HEART OF THE HIDE written inside a snorting steer stamped in the "DEEP WELL" POCKET. The TRIPLE ACTION web with a *Spiral Top* (in grade-school cursive). Along the thumb, Rawlings's familiar bright-red Circle R. Next to it, another classic, the EDGE-U-CATED HEEL. Below that, the patent number, 2,995,757. (And below that, my first initial and last name. And a single, mysterious black dot.) Along the glove's heel, XPG6 stamped just above the handsome Rawlings script, with a long, swooping tail on the R, itself resting atop the letters U.S.A. Only the U and the top of the S are discernible today.

Two other marks cemented my love. Explanation is unnecessary as to why, arcing along the pinkie, FOR THE *Professional* PLAYER was so seductive. The signature's allure was less obvious. My glove was endorsed by Willie Stargell, who (a) threw lefthanded and (b) played 111 games at first base in 1976. Why his autograph—which looked fake, with penmanship-class loops and flourishes—was on what I assumed was a middle infielder's glove was incomprehensible, but I loved its cocktail-conversation quality. When you're fourteen, weird sometimes is good.

It's not a stretch to say that I've had a longer (and closer) relationship with my baseball glove than anyone or anything, apart, maybe, from my immediate family and a couple of childhood pals. I broke it in in the manner of the times: a couple of baseballs, string, the underside of my mattress, ceaseless play. It carried me through my last two years of organized ball, on a team sponsored by the local American Legion post.

A black-and-white team photo hangs framed on my office wall now. It's from the end of the 1977 season, and of the eighth grade. I sit smiling in the front row

of wooden bleachers along the first-base line at Glover Field with my friends Peter Derby (shortstop), John McNamara (leftfield), and Chuck Heaphy (rightfield, coach's son), and a younger kid whose name I can't remember. My wavy hair wings out from under the two-tone cap with the too-high crown. Black block felt letters spell LEGION across the chests of our double-knit uniforms. We wear what are essentially Detroit Tigers period road grays: black, orange, and white piping along the neck and sleeves of the buttonless jerseys, black stirrups with orange and white stripes stretched as high as possible to reveal as much of our white sanitary socks as possible. The Seventies rocked.

The XPG6 rests on my left knee. My index finger pokes out, pointing directly at the camera lens. The leather is dark and rich. I am young and small. The twelve-inch XPG6 is new and large—much too large for me, a glove worn, I have since learned, by big-league outfielders and third basemen. Joe Morgan used a ten-inch glove at second base at the time. But what did I know? (More relevant: what did the salesman know?) All that matters is that, in that photograph, the XPG6 and I look like we're starting life, which, of course, we are.

How did it do for me? Records of my glove's rookie year are lost to history. But my 1978 Legion season is preserved on a single piece of lined white loose-leaf paper, folded inside a schedule, stored with other keepsakes in the basement. It reveals that I played in 13 games—with 9 appearances at second base, 4 at shortstop, and a few innings at third base and in rightfield—and committed 5 errors, 2 of them in our 9-4 championship-game loss to Cornell Carpet. (The stat sheet also shows that I totaled just 4 hits in 23 at-bats, an average of, ouch, .175. But that I walked 16 times and had a robust on-base percentage of .404. Billy Beane would have given me a chance.)

I can still see and feel the ball rolling under the XPG6, and through my legs, during tryouts for the junior varsity the next spring, ending my competitive hardball career. But my glove's best years were yet to come. In college, on fast but honest artificial turf at the University of Pennsylvania's historic Franklin Field, my glove snared line drives, grabbed one-hoppers to the shortstop side, shielded me from screaming bullets, and started more 1-6-3 double plays than you'd expect. My team won back-to-back intramural softball championships, and my glove was one of the stars. Later, it performed well on the pitcher's mound again in New York City softball leagues. It shagged hundreds of baseball fungoes lofted heavenward on lazy afternoons by my best friend Jon.

As I aged—knee surgeries, work, a wife and daughter—my glove lay dormant most springs and summers, its color fading and leather peeling: wan, weathered, cracked. But it's always remained in sight, not stashed in a closet or buried in a box of moldering sports equipment. Single, on a couch, in Brooklyn, the Yankees on TV—married, in Washington, in the attic, at a desk—I put on the XPG6 and whip a ball into its still-perfect pocket. My glove is a comfort.

● ● ●

My glove was manufactured in 1976 in Willow Springs, Missouri. It is made of tanned steer hide, specifically Code 5 Horween-X Catcher's Mitt Glove Leather from the Horween Leather Company in Chicago, founded in 1905. The exterior leather is 0.075 inch thick and cut from a durable two-foot stretch along the steer's backbone, the heart of the hide. The separate interior, a glove within the glove known as the lining, is 0.050 inch thick and hails from the softer belly. The web comes from the butt, the toughest part of the hide. Rawlings doesn't have a slogan for that.

I know all of this because Bob Clevenhagen tells me. To establish my glove's birth year, for instance, Bob has me look on the outside of the thumb, below the patent number. How many dots?

"One dot," I say.

"One dot. That's exactly right. Made in 1976. But it wouldn't have gone out in the marketplace until the first of 1977."

I'd noticed the one-sixteenth-inch dot years ago but had no idea what it meant. I thought it was an accidental factory mark. Bob explains that Rawlings used dots to establish the year of manufacture for warranty purposes. One dot meant a glove was made in a year ending in 1 or 6, two dots was a year ending in 2 or 7, and so on. That way, if someone returned a glove for repair or replacement, Rawlings would know whether it was still under warranty (and the owner would have no idea how the company could tell).

After working at shoe factories in Missouri and Massachusetts, Bob joined Rawlings as foreman of glove operations in Willow Springs in 1977. ("Leather was my life after I got out of the service," he says.) A workforce of two hundred made about

170,000 gloves there that year, including 15,000 or so XPG6s. As Rawlings and other glove makers began shifting production to Asia, the Willow Springs factory was closed in 1982. Today, Bob runs a four-person operation at Rawlings's main distribution center in Washington, Missouri, making gloves for a couple dozen major leaguers and for a custom catalogue.

The XPG6 and its progenitors were Rawlings's first fully functional modern gloves, created in response to Wilson's A2000, which revolutionized baseball when it appeared in 1957. The A2000 had a larger web, broader pocket, hinged heel, and flatter fingers, thumb, and heel than the standard puffy models of the time. In his artful book *Glove Affairs: The Romance, History, and Tradition of the Baseball Glove,* Noah Liberman explains that the A2000 dispelled a century-old belief: that the glove should look like the hand. "The evolution of the glove is, in large part," he writes, "the slow realization that a glove must reflect how a hand moves to catch a ball, not how it looks when you stare at it." (Liberman and I, it turns out, have something in common, glove-wise. "The XPG6? That was my glove!" he exclaims when I call. "That was my glove in high school!" Liberman swapped his with the shortstop of a women's pro baseball team for a jersey. She never sent him the shirt.)

Rawlings began making XPG prototypes—the initials stood for "experimental glove"—for big-league players in 1958. The first retail model, the XPG3, endorsed by pitcher Herb Score, appeared in the company's 1960 catalogue. The quarter-inch shorter but otherwise identical XPG6 debuted in 1962 and quickly became one of Rawlings's most popular gloves. The autograph inside helped: Mickey Mantle. According to glove historian Dennis Esken—who owns the glove Mantle used to make a one-handed catch in left-centerfield that helped preserve Don Larsen's perfect game in the 1956 World Series—the model name bore a "6" because it originally was intended for Stan Musial, who wore that number. For Mantle, Rawlings designed an XPG7, but, Esken tells me, the famous No. 7 didn't like it. It had a newfangled Trap-Eze web with a vertical strip of leather connected to each side with laces; the Mick wanted a solid web. Since Musial was nearing the end of his career anyway, Rawlings put Mantle's name in the XPG6.

The original XPG6 was a "Personal Model," meaning the pattern of the glove, if not every detail of the glove itself, was the same as what the signer wore on the field. (Mantle wound up using an I-shaped web, as opposed to the two-piece Triple

Action web in the retail version.) Mantle retired in 1968, but his name remained in the XPG6 until 1972. Bobby Tolan, a lefthanded outfielder on Cincinnati's Big Red Machine, endorsed the XPG6 in 1973 and 1974. (Lefty signatures on righty gloves aren't unusual; glove makers don't sell enough lefties to segregate endorsers by throwing arm.) Then came Stargell. The future Hall of Famer had played in the outfield his entire career, but in 1975, the first year he signed the XPG6, he moved to first base. My glove was stitched in 1976, Stargell's name was shifted to a first base-man's glove (the FJ9) in 1977, and the XPG6 name was retired.

I tell Bob I think it's the ideal design.

"From a baseball standpoint, I agree with you," he says, quickly noting that he didn't design it. Credit for that goes to the late Rollie Latina, who in 1961 inherited the title of Glove Designer from his father, Harry, better known as Doc, as in the Glove Doctor, who joined Rawlings in 1922. The Latinas were the revered creators of most of the company's trademarked glove innovations and slogans. Bob became Glove Designer after Rollie retired in 1984. The shape of the pattern and the shape of the padding, Bob says, predisposed the XPG6 to excellence. "It's the perfect shape to play it anywhere you want to play it. Bill Madlock wore it at third base. Dwight Evans wore it for fourteen years in the outfield. That glove's been every-where."

Tom Seaver, Hank Aaron, Mike Schmidt, Billy Williams, Doug DeCinces—I shared a glove with them, too, I learn. "It was the first, most-streamlined model with that U-shaped heel and that nice pocket in it and a little less padding in it. It's more like what we use today," Bob says. "That same glove is still around. The truth is that it's the very same basic pattern. A-Rod's wearing it today," he says, referring to Yan-kees third baseman Alex Rodriguez. There are some differences, Bob notes. A-Rod's glove has a single-piece "Fastback" backside with a "Holdster" for the index finger. "The palm area. That's where it's the same as A-Rod, Dwight Evans, right back to Mickey Mantle."

Esken, the historian and collector, puts it to me this way. "Fifty freakin' years. That pattern glove has been synonymous with baseball for fifty years. It's still func-tional to this date. The A2000 from 1957 is not a functional glove today."

● ● ●

Bob has made gloves for Presidents Carter, Ford, and both Bushes. He has made gloves for movies—Kevin Costner's *For Love of the Game, The Slugger's Wife,* written by Neil Simon, Billy Crystal's *61*.* After the comedian paid $239,000 at a Sotheby's auction for a glove supposedly worn by Mantle circa 1960, he asked Bob to check it out. Bob could tell, based on the style of Mantle's signature, it was a 1965 model (an XPG3). "I could have saved him a lot of money in ten seconds," he says.

At sixty-two years old, Bob is one of Rawlings's longest-serving employees, and its de facto glove historian, fielding questions from reporters, fans, even investigators. The FBI once called about a 1936 Joe DiMaggio rookie gamer sold by a prominent auction house. It actually had been made two decades later, after DiMaggio had retired. "Some of the experts who write letters, they don't know shit," Bob tells me. "But it doesn't take a brain surgeon to know a '36 glove from a '54 glove." One day when I call, Bob is making a glove for a boy missing some fingers whose parents wrote requesting help. (He made gloves for one-handed big-league pitcher Jim Abbott.) "I get four or five of those a year," he says. "We don't advertise or charge for it. I just do it for a nice letter from the kid. I've got a nice little file of those."

Most big leaguers, Bob says, don't know much about their gloves. "They don't even know what the hell they're getting. They get oil-tanned leather. It's going to be darker from day one. Probably the last person who knows how to make a glove is a pro ballplayer. . . . They've got a lot of bad habits. They spit in 'em. That just rots the leather. Makes it feel sticky. It just ruins the glove." (I don't confess that I regularly spit in the XPG6, but only because those big leaguers did.) "They don't care today. It doesn't take another year to break another one in."

Today's pros, Bob says, want supple leather right out of the box. They don't want to have to work it in. Players like Dwight Evans who wear the same glove for an entire career are as rare as perfect games. Modern players burn through multiple gloves in a season; Bob pounds and shapes gloves for Alex Rodriguez six at a time. Of course he does. It's good for business.

"Who wouldn't want A-Rod wearing their glove on TV?" Bob says. "What's a lousy dozen gloves?" Compare that to the old days. "We wouldn't even give Stan Musial an extra glove in the Fifties. If he wanted another one he'd have to buy it."

Bob goes on. "These players are much different from your era." The "your era" is simultaneously flattering (I lived in the old days? And there was something good about them?) and horrifying (It wasn't that long ago, was it?). "They don't care about durability."

They do care about the endorsement money—$100,000 or so a year for an A-Rod or Derek Jeter—but they don't need it the way players did back in the day. Bob estimates Willie Stargell probably received "$5,000 and a set of golf clubs" to sign with Rawlings, plus royalties on sales above $5,000. "It mattered back then," Bob says. "I know Reggie Jackson made as much off us as he did playing ball. The Mantles of the world had to have a winter job to eat. I'm pretty sure A-Rod doesn't have to check in at Hardee's after the season's over."

• • •

On a bright afternoon two months into the 2006 season, my glove and I drive to Robert F. Kennedy Stadium—one year older than the XPG6—where the Washington Nationals are hosting the Houston Astros.

I collect my press pass and fast-walk to the home dugout. It stinks of sewage, thanks to some faulty piping manager Frank Robinson hopes the team's just-named owners will see fit to repair. As his players take batting practice, Robinson holds court with a clutch of reporters. He complains about how players won't accept instruction. He says they arrive in the big leagues sure they know everything. He outs slackers on his team by name. Of course, he does all of this off the record. Praise is on the record, though, because Frank Robinson loves and respects the game and loves and respects those who do, too.

When the beat guys finish their questions, I extract the XPG6 from my messenger bag. Everyone eyes me a bit warily—I'm not a regular, and I'm breaking the sportswriters' code of conduct by behaving weirdly in front of the people wearing uniforms. When he sees the glove, Robinson's expression falls somewhere between shame and disgust.

"You should be brought up on abuse charges," he says. "You ever oil that thing?" Well, no, but I did have it restrung about ten years earlier, when the X-shaped lacing between the middle and index fingers broke.

"You don't even want to touch it," I say.

"No."

The manager asks who signed it, and I launch into an exegesis of the XPG6's family tree.

"Why would they change the Mickey Mantle model?" he asks. "Because he was retired," I say.

"So what?" Robinson says. "I'll tell you what. If they would have kept Mickey Mantle's name on that they would have sold more gloves than they would have with Bobby Tolan's name."

Ice broken, the other reporters join in. One asks Robinson, who won a Gold Glove in 1958, about his glove preferences. He tells us he used only a few in his twenty-one-season career. "Gloves are like shoes with me," he says. "I find a pair of shoes I like, I wear 'em. You just had a glove that felt good on your hand, you didn't quit playing with it."

Bill Mazeroski's glove was tattered, Robinson recalls. Willie Mays's glove was "beyond limit," he says. "It looked like those things they play jai alai with." Players couldn't be picky. "There were no specifications. They showed you models of gloves and you chose one that you liked." Robinson says he first signed with MacGregor, but didn't like the gloves, so he switched to Rawlings and wore a Spalding occasionlly.

Talk returns to my XPG6.

"That's the kind of glove you'd see guys playing with," he says. "Restrung, re-done, whatever."

I take this as a compliment, but seek a higher order of validation. "Do you like the shape at least?" I ask Robinson. "Say something nice about my glove. You're killing me."

"It's on your hand. It's not bad. How long have you had it?" "Thirty years."

"It's not bad. It's not too bad. It's got a nice kind of shape for an infielder's glove."

But Frank Robinson thinks I need to move on.

"Get a softball glove," he says. "Retire that one."

"I can't retire it."

"Why not?"

"Because I love it."

"Sleep with it. But you don't have to abuse it. I love my wife but I leave her to come to work."

"I've had a longer relationship with my glove than I have with my wife." "That's you. The way you're going with that glove, you're not going to know your wife much longer."

Across the infield, I wait for the Astros to finish batting practice. As the pitchers jog in from the outfield, where they've been shagging balls, I look for No. 36, Russ Springer.

Springer, Rawlings has informed me, is the only player in the major leagues using the XPG6, albeit under a different name, the Pro 6XBC. That model was also discontinued years ago, but the company makes him a couple every year. When Springer arrives at the dugout railing, I introduce myself. I tell him what we have in common, and he says he likes our glove because he played infield in high school and so prefers a smaller model (smaller for him, that is; he's six-feet-four). In his native Louisiana twang, Springer says the glove he's holding isn't his gamer, which is stashed in his locker. "It don't come out unless it's game time," he says.

Springer has used the same glove in games since 1993, his second year in the majors. "It's starting to show a lot of wear and tear," he says. "Sun-bleached on the outside. It's starting to get a couple of tears on it. The only thing I've ever had done is have the top laces replaced, all through the fingers. Just to show you how old it is, and yours is too, they don't make 'em with metal rivets anymore. And mine's still got the metal rivets. You'll see mine. It's a lot like that."

He gives my glove a once-over, examining the pocket.

"Mine actually looks worse in here than yours does."

"Can we go compare?" I ask.

"Yeah."

"Let's go."

We walk into the visitors' clubhouse and over to Springer's locker. A few days earlier, the righthanded reliever had been suspended for four games for throwing at Barry Bonds, possibly because Bonds had 713 home runs at the time and Springer didn't want to give up No. 714, possibly to let Bonds know how he felt about alleged steroids-using sluggers. (After throwing one pitch behind Bonds's back and three more inside, Springer plunked Bonds on the right shoulder and was ejected from the game. As he exited the field, Springer received a standing ovation from the home crowd.) I tell Springer our glove originally was worn by Mickey Mantle, which elicits no response. Not a historian, I guess. He pulls his gamer from the locker.

His Pro 6XBC has the crosshatched (and trademarked) Basket Web.

Instead of "DEEP WELL" POCKET, Springer's glove is stamped with GOLD GLOVE. His also doesn't have an EDGE-U-CATED HEEL. His red rectangular Rawlings label on the wrist strap says "Made in U.S.A."; mine says "Est. 1887." Springer's glove is broken in a bit flatter than mine. Otherwise, they are identical: same shape, same stitch patterns, same lace holes, same curves, same feel.

"So when you look at something like this"—I hold up the XPG6—"you don't think: old piece of leather?"

"Heck no," he says. "That's personality."

Springer says he's a creature of habit. He wears the same spikes all season. His black batting practice T-shirt (featuring his once and future teammate Roger Clemens) has a giant hole around the underarm. "I just don't like new stuff," he says.

When it comes to our glove, I tell him, I'm the same way. "I was a kid when I got it," I say. "I played softball with it for twenty years, so it's a little bit fatter and wider. But you could play with this? You wouldn't have a problem putting this on?"

"No, that's got personality," he says. "It's better than a new one."

• • •

"You need a little TLC on it," Craig Biggio says.

We're sitting on metal folding chairs on the other side of the Astros' locker room. The second baseman holds my glove gently, his thick fingers resting just beneath the wrist strap, but not inserted into the slots. "Never put your hand totally into someone else's glove," he says. Indeed, I always avoided lending my glove. The borrower inevitably would, to my horror, stick his index finger *inside* it. A few months earlier, I'd shown my glove to Cal Ripken, Jr., who, as if testing me, inserted his hand and *then* admonished that I "should have been more territorial with it." Ripken said the only person he had ever allowed to use his gamer was Ronald Reagan, when the president threw out a first pitch in 1984. (Of the XPG6, the future Hall of Fame shortstop/third baseman said, and I proudly quote, "You break yours in similar to me.")

Bob Clevenhagen had recommended talking to Biggio, who won four consecutive Gold Gloves in the 1990s and, more important, appreciates the art of the glove. "It's what you make your money with," Biggio says. "A lawyer goes to work with a nice suit on every day. We've got to put a glove on our hands. If you don't know how to use it, you're not going to have a job very long. It is personal. And everybody's different."

Biggio uses one glove per season. He's a throwback, preferring firmer leather that requires attention and work on the part of the owner. But he says he's not an extremist. Steve Buechele, a third baseman for Texas, Pittsburgh, and the Cubs, used one glove his entire career, Biggio tells me, as did journeyman shortstop Jay Bell. Oakland shortstop Walt Weiss's glove was so ravaged it had a nickname: The Creature. Biggio says the great Cardinals shortstop Ozzie Smith took the opposite approach. He could remove a new glove from its box and play with it the same day. "But he had some of the best hands ever," Biggio says.

Biggio does more work on his gloves than Smith did, but not much more. Bob sends the nineteen-year veteran a few gloves before spring training. Biggio picks a future gamer and plays catch with it. He puts a little pine tar in the pocket for "tackiness," which he says helps in cold weather when the ball is slicker. By the start of the regular season, the glove is ready. By the end, the fingers have stretched just enough to force its retirement. Biggio gives the old ones to his two sons. "They can't wait to get this one," he says, showing me his Pro CB (his initials), which is similar to the XPG6 but smaller. "It seems like a good one right now."

Like a diamond cutter appraising a stone, Biggio studies my glove. I ask what he sees.

"It's got a story to it," Biggio says. "Classic, old, beat-up. This is a classic glove of somebody who would use it every day, who wouldn't change it at all. It's got a lot of character."

"Thank you," I say. Craig Biggio understands.

"For me, the pocket's a little deep," he continues, "so it's more like a third base-man's glove. But actually, it's not all that bad. If [the ball] goes in it, I *know* it's not coming out. I'd have the whole thing restrung." His glove has extra laces connecting the sides of the fingers to minimize separation between them. "The leather's a little dry." He points to the pocket and fingers. "That can be padded. They can patch it up."

Biggio tells me to send my glove to Bob.

"He'll fix it up for you."

• • •

Bob tells me what he'd do to restore my glove. "It needs new insides and new leather trim all the way around on the inside. And new laces, of course."

The trim curves around the wrist and fingers, holding together the pieces of my glove. Bob says he'll replace the interior lining—the glove within the glove, against which my palm and fingers, back and front, have rested since I was fourteen—with the same durable Horween leather as in the original, not the softer stuff pros and amateurs expect today. ("It took a man to break it in," he says of the glove of yore.) The challenge will be making the new lining fit snugly inside the old exterior; since leather stretches with use, the original pattern for the innards of the XPG6, which Bob has, probably won't match the current size of my glove.

In short, Bob says he will rebuild my glove from the inside, "everything under-neath that you can't see." On the undersides of the three middle fingers, he'll install fresh wool-blend padding (minus the asbestos fibers it contained thirty years ago). Beneath the wrist strap, a synthetic wool will take over for the old shearling. The two frayed red Rawlings labels—the rectangular script Rawlings and the Circle R—will be replaced with modern likenesses. "I don't have any more of these antique ones," he says. *Antique!* The exterior will remain unchanged; if he replaced that, Bob says, he'd just be making a new glove.

Letting the XPG6 out of my possession had been traumatic. I first packed it at the post office, but decided I didn't trust the government, unpacked it, and shipped it FedEx. I called Bob to make sure it arrived. I had wanted Bob's expert opinion, assuming that perhaps he would offer to string some new lacing or perform some trick to revive the worn leather. I hadn't considered a total makeover. But now, listening to him explain the restoration process like an archaeologist entrusted with preserving the Parthenon, I grow excited at the prospect of new life. I tell myself I finally would be treating the XPG6 right. I finally would be making amends for years of what Frank Robinson called abuse. Spontaneously, unhesitatingly, I give Bob the go-ahead.

"I don't think you'll be upset with the way it looks," he says.

• • •

A few weeks later, a brown box arrives. I pull out the XPG6 and say, aloud: Oh. *No!*

It's my glove, but it isn't. It stays open of its own accord, rather than flopping shut on release, the tip of the thumb kissing the tip of the pinkie. The finger slot no longer lies permanently in the off position, pancaked to the lining. I slide my hand in. The XPG6 is snug and stiff. I can't even close it enough to obscure Stargell's too-neat signature.

The insides are burnt sienna, rich with the aroma of new leather. The laces and trim Bob had promised are bright and prominent, mod orange racing stripes on a battered Chevrolet. The replacement Rawlings patches shimmer like freshly washed fire engines drying in the summer sun. The spongy synthetic wool rubs prominently against the back of my hand; I can't even recall feeling the old stuff, tamped as it was. New internal padding forms a thick ridge along the index, middle, and ring fingers, functionally useful but interrupting the pocket's old, uniform concavity. There's even a bump in the new leather exactly where the top of my thumb rests. An imperfection! Bob, how could you?

I feel disappointment and then panic: I'll never again hold *my glove,* the one that accompanied me through adolescence and into adulthood, a life partner whose

advancing years were undetectable because we had aged together, an anti–Dorian Gray. I didn't want a trophy wife. But now I have one.

For a second time, I feel like I'm going to cry because of my baseball glove. The XPG6 was comforting because it was so familiar. It had earned its cracks and bruises on the field, over time. Holding the remodeled version, I close my eyes and picture my glove, trying to imprint permanently its sensory qualities on my brain. How I could make the upper half flap by snapping my wrist back and forth. How I could wield it like a lobster's claw to snatch a ball off the ground. Its gloriously battered and decomposing personality, in Russ Springer's apt anthropomorphization. Even if my preschool daughter becomes a softball superstar, there's no chance I'll play enough to return the XPG6 to its old form—not enough throws to catch, not enough grounders to field, not enough time. I feel I've committed a horrible betrayal. I set down the imposter and vow not to pick it up until I'm emotionally willing to give it a chance.

• • •

The pain begins to lift a month later. What made the XPG6 special was its artistry, I realize, its shape, form, and feel. The essence of those remains unchanged. In fact, the shape and form are truer, the parabola stronger and more confident. Propped upright, resting on its wrist strap, the XPG6 reminds me of the Gold Glove trophy itself. Its new contrast, I realize, is beautiful: I. M. Pei's glass pyramid at the Louvre.

More than I have in years, I bang the pocket with my right fist, flattening the new padding. I grab the pinkie and ring finger in my right hand and open and close the glove to resuscitate its natural hinge. With my left thumb, I push and flatten the bump under my thumb (caused, I guess correctly, by the difference in size between the XPG6's lining pattern and my stretched-out glove) to which I'm sure Bob was referring in the note that accompanied the glove home: "I wish it was a little better! But!! Good Luck, Bob."

Inside the box, Bob deposited the battered core of the XPG6. It looks like something that's been worn since Honus Wagner was playing shortstop. The leather is as weather-beaten as a cowboy's chaps. Waxy remnants of the grease that affixed the lining to the glove's exterior form a dark, mottled circle on the palm. Where the fleshy part of my heel rested and sweated, there's a hole the size of a half dollar and the shape of Wisconsin, and a tear next to that. The padding beneath the three middle fingers is shredded. At the point where the nail of my ring finger touched the leather, there's another hole—the result of untold thousands of repetitions of finger sliding into glove, right fist pounding left hand, balls batted and thrown striking that precise spot.

Then, finally, there's the index finger slot, pressed as flat as a stone made for skipping across a lake. I peek underneath. The leather is smooth, dark, unblemished, my glove in 1977. Still with me today, still perfect.

I'm going to use my new glove as much as possible. What's left of my glove—My Glove—I'm having framed.

Stefan Fatsis writes about sports for the *Wall Street Journal* and talks about them on National Public Radio's *All Things Considered*. He is the author of the best-seller *Word Freak: Heartbreak, Triumph, Genius, and Obsession in the World of Competitive Scrabble Players* and *Wild and Outside: How a Renegade Minor League Revived the Spirit of Baseball in America's Heartland*. His latest book is *A Few Seconds of Panic: A 5-Foot-8, 170-Pound, 43-YearOld Sportswriter Plays in the NFL*, published by Penguin Press.

MY BRILLIANT CAREER

Susan Perabo

Why is there so much written about baseball? Why do writers—even fiction writers, like me— feel compelled to weigh in on the subject? As with love, the topic is inexhaustible because it feels like personal property to everyone who holds the sport dear. As with love, there is always something new— something original, something crucial—to add to the conversation.

This past summer I went to see my St. Louis Cardinals play the Washington Nationals at RFK Stadium. Turns out, when a batter approaches the plate at RFK, not only do his stats appear on the jumbotron but also his date of birth. Now, I'd come to terms some time ago with the fact that I'm considerably older than a lot of major league players. Albert Pujols has only a few years on the kids in my creative writing classes. Kerry Wood, A-Rod, Renteria—I might have babysat them. But it was a most unpleasant surprise when Jim Edmonds came to bat and I was informed in five-foot-high letters of his date of birth: 6/27/70. I literally blinked to clear my vision—those lighted numbers get blurry sometimes in the glare of a night game. I had always thought of Edmonds as the old man of the team, the seasoned vet, the big brother (*my* big brother), the guy who could put things into perspective and buy you a frozen Coke afterwards. Could it possibly be that I was *older* than Edmonds? And yet the numbers, when I looked again, were the same. My big brother had, in an instant, become my little brother. And in the next instant the sobering truth came clear: it was nearly time for me to retire.

Retiring from a pretend baseball career is more difficult than a nonpretend baseball player might imagine. My career, though entirely imagined, has been long and rewarding. Am I a superstar? Far from it. Even in my fantasy life some tenuous grip on reality must be maintained. My lifetime average is .268; my fielding percentage is regularly among those of the top five second basemen in the league; I once won a Gold Glove; one season my on-base percentage was so high I was moved to second in the order; I played in one All-Star Game (purely for the sake of novelty . . . I know when I'm the ballplayer and when I'm *the girl*) and I hit a double down the rightfield line that scored the go-ahead run for the National League; I got tossed from a game for arguing a called strike; I'm too slow to steal, but I'm the worst kind of pest on the base paths; I once tumbled into the stands to catch a foul ball; I'm always the first to the ballpark.

A friend who knows of my pretend career recently asked me if I thought a woman would ever play major league baseball. You might think I would have mulled over this question considerably in the course of my career, but you'd be wrong. Once it became clear *I* would not be the first woman stepping onto the diamond at Busch or Wrigley or Fenway, I went about the business of baseball fandom and my pretend career and have not worried much about the state of women in the game. But perhaps, with my pretend retirement on the pretend horizon, this is the perfect time to consider the question.

One thing's for certain: my *personal* glass ceiling had nothing to do with gender and everything to do with talent. When I played college baseball I was the backup second baseman for a team so new—it had turned from a club sport to a varsity team just the season before—there were no tryouts; I made the team by showing up at the organizational meeting. Barring divine intervention (not that I didn't consider this a real possibility for a good while), it was clear my actual baseball career would and should begin and end with my beloved Webster University Gorlocks. But of course there have been other women since who have played at the collegiate level, in programs far more established than my own. The best known is Julie Croteau. Sometimes referred to as the first woman to play NCAA baseball (I'm mostly over this), she started at first base for St. Mary's College, went on to become the first

woman to coach college baseball, and eventually played for the Colorado Silver Bullets, a professional women's baseball team that played against professional men's teams for five years in the 1990s. Croteau is now affiliated with the American Women's Baseball Federation, an organization that promotes women's amateur baseball. Was Julie Croteau good enough to play in the majors? She was not. How about Ila Borders, who pitched for three years in the Northern League in the late '90s? She neither, nor the often overlooked Toni Stone, who played in the Negro Leagues in the early '50s. But were these women the cream of the crop?

The answer is no. With all respect to these women, they were not the best of the best. The best of the best, I firmly believe, are lost before they are found. They are discouraged by well-meaning parents, steered in other directions. Billie Jean King once dreamed of playing big league baseball, but was encouraged by her parents (thank goodness, we must think now) to pursue tennis instead. Most girls who love baseball are, of course, steered to softball, and the fact is, at the earliest level—the elementary school level—the two sports are fairly interchangeable. The softball used for young girls is smaller than a regulation softball, just slightly bigger than a base-ball; it can be driven, thrown, and fielded almost exactly like a baseball. The size of the field, the distance between bases, the speed of the pitches (often thrown by coach-es)—all these are very similar, at first. But when the size of the ball changes (usually when girls are around twelve), the whole game begins to change; softball gradually becomes a game of small-ball, of bunts and infield hits, of manufacturing runs with a huge ball on a tiny field. What had once been nearly interchangeable with baseball becomes, by high school, an entirely different sport, and a young woman hoping to shift from softball to baseball might as well be trying to shift from soccer to football. Besides, a star player on her high school softball team may have her eyes fixed on a scholarship to play college softball, and why would she give that up to play a sport in which she has no future? And what adolescent athlete wants to have to wage a battle against the status quo? Being a teenage girl is difficult enough; who wants to be the girl who's *different*? The girl who may even have to sue her high school to be allowed to play with the guys? (Julie Croteau tried this, without success.) Gina Satriano, another former Silver Bullet, told *The Sporting News:* "We had to fight to play Pony League, we had to fight to play Colt League. When I got to high school, Mom asked me if I wanted to fight to play there, too, and I said, 'I'm tired of fighting. I just want to play.' So I played softball. I just didn't enjoy the game as much." Lest it seem I'm demonizing a wonderful sport, I must point out that softball—which became widely popular in large part due to Title IX—has given countless girls and women opportunities they would never have had otherwise. But it's also been a convenient way to keep young girls out of baseball.

So we come to the sticky question: even if the best women did play baseball, would they be able to compete with the best men? The answer's even stickier: no way. The physical differences between men and women are too vast. Asked about the possibility of women playing major league baseball, Babe Ruth said, "They will never make good. Why? Because they are too delicate. It would kill them to play ball every day." As was often the case, the lovable old pig missed the point entirely. The problem is one not of endurance, but of physical strength (primarily upper body strength) and speed. In no sport is the best woman better or faster than the best man. And the numbers are drastically against us. Say one in ten thousand men have the natural ability that—with the best coaching and the right attitude—could take them to the majors. The numbers for women? Maybe one in one hundred thousand. Couple those staggering odds with the early social pressures to play a "girl's game" rather than a boy's, and it's pretty clear why the gender barrier has not yet been broken.

But, as we all say when we buy the Powerball ticket despite the enormous odds: well, *somebody's* got to win, right? Indeed, even if the odds of a woman playing in the bigs are one in a million, it's logical to assume that the one can't be too far off. And the more girls play baseball, the more the odds are with us. The American Women's Baseball Federation, with Julie Croteau and other former Silver Bullets on board, is seeking to bring women into the game earlier, offering baseball camps for girls only and holding regional, national, and international baseball tournaments for young women. It will take opportunities like this, and a powerful parental influence, to create the first woman major leaguer. There's no doubt in my mind that had Richard Williams decided to groom his daughters into baseball players rather than tennis players, at least one of them—probably Serena—would have had the ability to play in the majors.

So here's my fearless prediction: look for her in 2024, a control pitcher with great lower-body strength, a middle reliever with brilliant placement and dagger eyes. Or possibly a second baseman with quick hands and feet, a player with the skills I've honed in my pretend career: a contact hitter and excellent fielder with fierce determination. Mark it in pen on your calendar: she's coming soon(ish) to a dugout near you.

But for now, for today, there's only me: Susan Perabo, DOB: 1/6/69. Aaron and Mays played past forty, but I am no Aaron or Mays. I am not even an Edmonds. Some infield greats lose a step or two in their mid-thirties, but still manage to make amazing plays. But I don't have a step or two to lose. And my pretend average this year is five points lower than last, a trend I fear is irreversible, no matter how much time I spend in the gym or the cages during the off-season. Perhaps the dignified thing to do would be to retire. There's nothing worse than watching a ballplayer play one season too long, nothing worse than wondering "Doesn't she know it's over?"

But here's where the *pretend* part of my pretend career comes in handy. This winter, against all odds, my hours in the gym will pay off. And in the cages I'll find, inexplicably, that I'm seeing the ball a little better. Yes, my retirement still looms, but it now seems I have at least one more season left in these legs and hands and eyes. There's a bounce in my step, a fire in my belly, and my fingers grip invisible balls even as I sleep. I feel fresh. I feel young. I feel like . . . a girl.

Susan Perabo is writer-in-residence and an associate professor of English at Dickinson College. She is the author of *Who I Was Supposed to Be,* a collection of short stories, and *The Broken Places,* a novel.

FIELD OF DREAMS

George Plimpton

There probably aren't many writers who would volunteer to pitch in the majors. In fact, there's probably only one: George Plimpton, who, while sitting in the stands at a game in 1960, started to wonder what the view was like from the mound. His curiosity led him, as it did with football and boxing, to talk his way into the sport, and before the start of the 1960 All-Star Game, Plimpton faced the National League lineup. In this essay, written more than forty years later, Plimpton reflects on being put out to pasture, demoted over the years from the pitching mound to first base to rightfield. [L. G.]

I can't remember whether it was last summer, or the one before that, or maybe even three years ago, when, in a pickup baseball game after lunch, I was the last one picked. The captain, a teenager, referred to me as "Mister." He asked me if I would play rightfield. Sure, I said. I thought longingly of the half-finished glass of white wine back on the porch.

The others ran to their positions. The first baseman, a twelve-year-old, stretched out his length like a big leaguer to receive the warm-up tosses zipped across the infield.

There were two of us who walked to our positions—the young pitcher (a third my age), because that is in the nature of pitchers, and myself. Even in pickup softball games, pitchers move with a kind of smug, imperial elegance to the pitching mound. As for me, I walked out to rightfield because there was no need to hurry. I don't run much—perhaps a burst of speed to get to a subway door before it closes. I was without a glove that afternoon, unless I had been able to borrow one from the rightfielder on the other team, which was unlikely. That year, if I recall correctly, she was a young Romanian ballerina who'd never played baseball.

Rightfield is where nothing happens. In softball games, just about everyone, except the ultrasuave, bats righthanded and they tend to pull the ball, which means that the left side of the infield and outfield gets almost all the play. When on rare occasions lefthanded batters step up—I say they are ultrasuave because they are a minority and cause consternation—everyone shifts around to compensate. The centerfielder encroaches upon the quiet refuge of rightfield. When a fly ball drifts out, he moves in front of the right-fielder. "Mine," he calls out, not with any degree of urgency but in a muted, condescending way as if it were better that he helped out in this situation, very much like a Boy Scout guiding an elderly lady across a street.

So rightfield is where the inept and those who are getting on in years are sent. They nurse the injury of being the last picked. They trudge out there by the oak tree and turn around.

It has always been my contention that great thoughts have been generated in the lonely wastes of rightfield. I have no doubt that Albert Einstein was playing rightfield when he came up with the theory of relativity. So was George Gershwin when he suddenly hummed to himself the upward scale that provides the opening notes of "Rhapsody in Blue." Wasn't Woodrow Wilson playing rightfield when he came up with the concept of the League of Nations? Was not Edwin Hubble staring up into the heavens hoping a baseball would never materialize when the first inklings of the Big Bang theory came to mind? William Randolph Hearst dreamed up his newspaper empire playing rightfield in a softball game more than a century ago. Hugh Hefner was in rightfield when . . . well, you get the drift.

For me, it wasn't always like this. In high school, during college, at the Sunday games for years after graduation, in the grass field beyond the A&P, I affected a studied, nonchalant walk as I ventured to the pitcher's mound.

Then one year I was asked if I would play first base. "First?"

"Well, Tim is a pretty good pitcher."

"Tim? Who's Tim?"

"The young kid over there warming up."

"Oh."

And then that summer afternoon last year, or was it a year or so before, a glass of white wine left on the luncheon table, I found myself in rightfield.

There are many rightfields in our lives; the ones you find on athletic fields may just be the most obvious. The equivalent in touch football is the position of center. He is invariably the last person picked in the lineup.

What the centers hear in the huddle, usually from quarterbacks scrabbling the play in the grass, is this: "OK, Jack, you go long to the right, down toward the bushes; Penny, you go long on the other side and cut right behind Steve; Warren, you go down the middle, then cut for the sideline. Who's the center?"

"I am."

"OK, you center it on three, take five steps down and if everyone's covered I'll throw it to you."

So the center does this—the five steps, the turn, arms up plaintively. Nothing. On offense, it was possible to spend the entire afternoon taking those five steps, turning, and watching the ball arch far overhead on its way downfield.

In soccer, the equivalent of rightfield is being picked to play goal—the least active of the positions, and thus suitable for a boy (or girl), or someone's grandfather. The unlucky person stands in line, shifting worriedly from one foot to the other, hoping not to be the last picked. Upon that indignity, "Hey, Joe" or "Jill" or "Mister, you're the goalie, OK?" the chosen person then trudges to where the two piles of coats mark the goalposts.

If one has been picked for the better team, a whole chilly autumn afternoon can be spent standing between two piles of coats waiting for something to happen, some movement from the other end.

Shep Messing, a professional goaltender who played for the New York Cosmos, told me once that he whiled away such moments of inactivity by talking to the goalposts. He felt he had to talk to someone, not very serious stuff. He'd say things like "Be there when I need you."

I remember from my brief playing days as a goaltender with the Boston Bruins (as a participatory journalist) that when my team was attacking the other net, the expanse of ice in front of me was so vast, I could hardly make out what was going on at the opposite end. I wrote about it thus: "With the puck at the other end, it was not unlike standing at the edge of a mill pond, some vague activity at the opposite end almost too far to be discernible—could they be bass fishing out there?— but then suddenly the distant, aimless, waterbug scurrying became an oncoming surge of movement as everything—the players, sticks, the puck—starts coming on a direct line, almost as if a tsunami, that awesome tidal wave of the South Pacific, had suddenly materialized at the far end of the mill pond, and was beginning to sweep down toward one . . . a great encroaching wave full of things being borne along full-tilt—hockey sticks, helmets, faces with no teeth in them, those black, barrel-like hockey pants, the skates, and somewhere in there that awful puck."

Alas, that is the sort of thing that can happen to disturb one's reveries in rightfield—the thwack of the distant bat, the faces of the infielders suddenly turning as the bills of their cap tilt first upwards, then directly toward right-field where the ball is beginning the downward curve of gravity's rainbow. If the rightfielder thought to look, it would be the first time while standing out there he had seen the infielders' faces, now staring at him with horror; instead he is staring up transfixed, arms stiff as poles, reaching for the sky as if praying to an almighty being.

I had a friend who, while playing rightfield in a pickup game, was frightened by a ball hit his way and tumbled backward into a thicket. While extracting himself from the bushes, he was bitten by a bee, probably a yellow jacket. He turned out to be violently allergic and was hurried to a local hospital where he fell in love at first sight with the receptionist. This chance meeting quickly resulted in a marriage, which turned out to be a disaster. I never mentioned it when we had lunch on occasion years later, but I've often thought that if he had caught that long-ago fly ball he might have escaped a rather unfortunate five years of his life.

Peter, Paul & Mary had a song about playing rightfield, echoing all this:
Playing right field it's easy, you know,
You can be awkward And you can be slow That's why I'm here in right field
Just watching the dandelions grow.

Oddly, at the conclusion of the song, with the rightfielder daydreaming as usual ("I don't know the inning/I've forgotten the score"), a ball is hit his way that he actually catches! Startled by everyone suddenly yelling at him ("And I don't know what for"), he looks up and the baseball falls into his glove for an out! Poetic license indeed! Hyperbole! No rightfielder worthy of the tradition would catch a ball.

I once played briefly with a softball team many of whose players refused to catch the ball at all. It was not because of age. They were "The Penguins"—a team put together from members of the New York Philharmonic orchestra. Almost all of them depended upon their fingers for their livelihood. So if a ball was hit to a violin player in rightfield, he (or she) would turn and run alongside the ball until it stopped before picking it up and throwing it toward the infield. I don't recall that we ever won a game.

Of course, rightfielders go to bat—the enormous moment, perhaps three or four times an afternoon, when the focus is on you, so unlike the peace of the grass out by the oak tree. You hear the cries of encouragement, and then it's over, a soft liner to the shortstop, the heads turned as you walk back to the others ("Nice bat, Pops!").

So what's on my mind as I set out for rightfield and the oak tree beyond? Sometimes I remember the sphinx's famous riddle that befuddled so many who were devoured by the winged lion when they couldn't solve it. What had four legs in the morning, two at midday, and three in the evening? The answer (which Oedipus solved and in doing so, saved the city of Thebes): man, who crawls as a baby, walks upright in the prime of life, and supports himself with a cane when he's old. The three stations in softball, if one extends the metaphor, would start with pitching, then first base, and end with rightfield. Too melancholy a thought. Better to consider Alexander Pope—"to be swift is less than to be wise."

And besides, one can consider the great rightfielders who have occupied the same area—Roger Maris, Hank Aaron, Reggie Jackson, Al Kaline, Frank Robinson, Enos Slaughter, King Kong Keller, Mel Ott. The latter played rightfield for the New York Giants in the Polo Grounds, very often standing in what became known as Ott's Spot because the stands behind him ("The Porch") were so close that there wasn't much to do except turn and watch the home run balls sail overhead. And, of course, the great Babe Ruth played rightfield.

I turn to face the infield. The game has begun. A pop fly goes up. Was it caught by the shortstop? The third baseman? Who knows. It is time for reverie, and the mind begins to soar. . . .

(from Cigar Aficionado, March/April 2000)

George Plimpton (1927–2003) was the long-time editor of *The Paris Review* and the author of several books about competing in professional sports, among them *Paper Lion,* about training as a backup quarterback for the Detroit Lions, and *Out of My League,* about pitching against National League All-Stars in 1960.

THE SOUTHWORTHS

Michael Shapiro

I found out about Billy Southworth and his son by accident. I was doing research on baseball in wartime and wondered whether there was anyone in the big leagues whose connection to events in Europe and the Pacific extended beyond the papers and the radio. In 1942 the game and those playing it seemed removed from the seismic events of the day, as if baseball were a world apart—which is, of course, its beauty. Then I discovered the story of Billy Southworth and his son. Billy also had a daughter, Carol, and it was she who shared with me her brother's diary, which is the basis for this story. This is a baseball story, I suppose, but really, it is the story of a father and a son and the bond between them. It breaks my heart.

There are a lot of stories about baseball during World War II, and the more they are told the more they almost succeed in making those years sound like a foolish time, when a man with one arm played outfield for the St. Louis Browns and a fifteen-year-old pitched for the Reds. They played because most of the major leaguers had enlisted or been drafted, even the reluctant ones like Joe DiMaggio, who was said to be upset about the drop in pay. Only the old or very young or, in a baseball context, the infirm, remained, which perhaps explains why it was only in wartime that the Browns, who fielded a team of older players known to drink like fish, ever made it to the World Series.

These stories might suggest that the war touched the game deeply, but that really wasn't the case. A few weeks after Pearl Harbor, the owners and the commissioner, Kenesaw Mountain Landis, met to consider canceling play for the duration. President Roosevelt, however, suggested the games continue so that an anxious nation might have something besides the war to think and talk about. Considering that in its early stages the war did not go well for the Allies and there was ample reason to believe they might even lose, this was a wise idea.

The war did intrude upon the game. There were scrap iron drives at the ballparks and signs reminding people to buy war bonds. Attendance was down, even though

servicemen were admitted free of charge. The major leaguers, by and large, stuck around through the end of the 1942 season but were almost all gone by the spring of 1944. By then the teams had stopped traveling south for spring training in order to keep railroad cars free for the troops. Some major leaguers saw combat. Several were injured and were never the same again. Two little-known big leaguers died in battle. Many more spent the war playing exhibition games overseas.

Still, whatever the players were thinking and feeling about the war seldom made its way into clubhouse conversation. A rare exception was the case of Larry French, who pitched for the Brooklyn Dodgers and in the spring of 1942 reacted to the report that the Japanese had invaded his native California by telling Cliff Dapper,

the backup catcher, that he was going home to fight. Dapper would have gone with him, had the story turned out to be true.

More common was the sentiment conveyed in a story I heard from Marty Marion, the tall and skinny St. Louis Cardinal shortstop. I asked Marion how often his teammates talked about the war, considering they were all of draft age and might even have had friends or relatives in the service. Marion, by then an elderly man, recalled the first summer of the war well: The Cardinals were chasing the Brooklyn Dodgers—they'd begun August ten games out of first place and then went on a tear of historic proportions. "The war?" Marion said. "What war? We were in a pennant race." Yet there was at least one man in that clubhouse thinking about the war, even if he was not disposed to speaking about it. To speak about the war would have meant revealing something of his feelings, which was just not done. Billy Southworth, the Cardinals' manager, had a son, Billy, Jr., who was a captain in the Army Air Corps and who in the summer of 1942 was preparing to ship out.

The story of this father and son is the sort too seldom told when people talk about baseball in wartime. That is a shame, because more than most, their story captures the true and complex nature of life on the home front: people going about the business of their lives but pausing every hour to listen to the news; young men deemed unfit for service feeling too ashamed to come out of the house; mothers sitting and weeping on the always-made beds of their sons in uniform. Stories of the American home front tend to suggest that life consisted of little more than watering victory gardens, collecting scrap, suffering the occasional air raid drill, and reading about ration cheats in the paper. They too often leave out the terror. This was not the terror of an attack; that was over by 1943. Rather, it was the terror of the Western Union man bringing the worst news imaginable, the terror that came from walking past a neighbor's house and seeing a gold star affixed in the window and wondering when your turn would come. There were two kinds of people on the home front: those who had men in the service and those who did not. They might have been friends before the war, but for the duration they really didn't have much to talk about.

Billy Southworth had a son in the service. He also had a team in a pennant race. This left him to straddle the world of the war and a world where the war did not seem to exist. He spent the war doing what everyone with a son, husband, or brother in uniform did: he waited.

● ● ●

Billy Southworth, Jr., was a ballplayer. But unlike his father he did not make it to the major leagues. Instead, he had the distinction of being the first professional ballplayer to enlist. That he did so eleven months *before* Pearl Harbor made his act of bravery greater still. Billy, Jr., had been a well-regarded minor league prospect when, after spending the 1940 season with Toronto in the International League, he decided to sign up. His father had hoped Billy, Jr., might follow him to the big leagues, and tried to get him to change his mind. The story of their conversation was often told in the early days of the war, when America was finding itself hard-pressed for heroes.

Billy, Jr., the story went, came to his father to break the news.

His father asked him to reconsider.

The son replied that there were things more important than baseball. The following morning the father came to his son and said, "This is a beautiful day to enlist."

Maybe the conversation took place just this way, and maybe the sportswriters who told it were trying to get other young men to be like Billy South-worth, Jr., which was not necessarily a bad idea. Billy, Jr., was tall, wore a mustache, and looked like Clark Gable. He carried himself with the bearing of a young man who knew that other young men envied him because of the way young women looked at him. He was a heartbreaker. Some of the men with whom he served found him a little too full of himself, but then, once they got to know him, became his friends.

There were women who wanted to marry Billy, Jr. Though he did give the matter serious thought, he did not feel inclined, as others did, to rush to marry before he shipped out, so that he could leave knowing someone was waiting for him. He was not the sort of young man given to fretting and dark thoughts about the perilous future that awaited him. He seemed the least burdened of men and took to leadership as if it was a naturally occurring gift. He possessed a swagger and confidence that left his father, for one, a little bit in awe. He, for his part, thought his father was "a grand fellow."

They were as close as a father and son could be. His mother had left them when Billy, Jr., was still young. His father, who had played thirteen major league seasons, was by then managing in the minors. They spent the winters together and, when school let out, Billy, Jr., would join his father on the back-roads circuit. He was the batboy.

The elder Southworth had had his struggles. He had been a solid, if unspectacular, outfielder whose career was built not upon size or muscle but on grit. He was also something of an innocent to city life—in New York and later St. Louis—and his attempts to keep up with his harder-drinking teammates ended badly. He managed the Cardinals briefly in 1929 but was fired when he tried too hard to emulate the harsh and exacting ways of his mentor, the great Giants manager John McGraw. Southworth slipped out of the game, found work as a salesman, remarried, and then had his career resurrected by Branch Rickey, the teetotaling general manager of the Cardinals, who sent him back to the minors to manage after Southworth swore off the bottle. He made it back to the big club in 1941, a changed man. Gone was the out-of-character brutishness; he was still demanding, but in a far less abrasive way. He seldom raised his voice. The Cardinals that year barely lost out to the Dodgers for the National League pennant, and Southworth's comeback was all but complete.

In the meantime, his son had grown into a ballplayer of considerable promise. In 1939 he had been voted most valuable player in the Canadian-American League

after batting .342 for the Rome Colonels, a minor league team in upstate New York. He played the outfield, ran well, and possessed a strong throwing arm. In 1940, he batted .280 for Toronto, a step below the majors. But by the early winter of 1941, he was at Parks Air College in East St. Louis, Illinois, learning to fly planes that barely held together. His father had driven him there from their farm in Sunbury, Ohio, on New Year's Day. He had woken his son early that morning and helped him pack before they set off together on the long drive. They arrived at Parks at ten o'clock that night. "A quick handshake and I was off," Billy, Jr., later wrote.

That memory appeared in a July entry in the diary Billy, Jr., had decided to keep. The diary would be for his father, and was dedicated to him, too. This way, in addition to the letters home, his father would have a record of the time they spent apart.

The diary of Billy Southworth, Jr., is remarkable not so much for its content but in the way it captures the particular way men—especially baseball men, who have seldom been given to introspection—talk to and about eachother. On page after page, spread over weeks and months and years, Billy, Jr., logged the events of his days, beginning in the summer of 1942: flying barely airworthy B-17s over the Arizona desert, news of yet another training crash, tales of friends taking the marriage plunge, complaints about superior officers who in his view were anything but. But there is something more: baseball scores. All the while, Billy, Jr., chronicled his father's pennant race: "Cards won 3-1 from Pirates, 7-1/2 games back. My day off, worked all day yet did not fly." It is as if he were saying, I was thinking of Dad, all that time. He would write, "Must write to dad."

It was as if he were speaking to his father through his diary, but in the oblique way in which men of a certain sort convey their feelings. There was, for instance, a story of a two-day pass to visit his father in Chicago, where the Cardinals were playing the Cubs: "It sure was great to see him again. We talked til three or four in the A.M."

The Cardinals kept winning, and in his diary, Billy, Jr., grew ever more excited. "One more game in two to play will clinch the pennant . . . got a wonderful letter from dad today."

By October, Billy, Jr., who'd become something of a celebrity, was invited to fly over Sportsman's Park for the opening game of the 1942 World Series, which the

Yankees were favored to win. But after dropping the first game, the Cardinals swept the next four and with them, the championship. "October 5—will be a memorable day in the history of Southworth," Billy, Jr., wrote. "Dad proved that he was the best manager in baseball today. Wired him immediately after the game, congratulations."

They saw each other one more time before Billy, Jr., left for England. His unit had been transferred to Bangor, Maine. His father visited for five days and Billy, Jr., introduced him around. The elder Southworth signed autographs and wrote his name on his son's plane, *The Bad Check* (so dubbed because bad checks always come back). He also gave him the cap he had worn that season. Billy, Jr., had it rigged with extra wiring so he could wear it into combat. "He's the grandest guy that I know," he wrote. "Sure tired of this sitting around—I want to go to combat."

He would not have long to wait. Whatever thoughts and fears Billy Southworth had in all the many months his son flew combat missions over France and Germany he seemed to have kept to himself. But he followed the news of every mission. As a manager, Southworth was a stickler for lists; he kept running tabs on opponents as well as his players. As a father, he kept a running account of bombing runs, and with each letter from his son, crossed off all the missions that ended with his safe return.

His Cardinals won the National League pennant again in 1943, but lost the World Series to the Yankees. They won again in 1944, and this time defeated the Browns in the one and only all–St. Louis World Series. His son, meanwhile, kept his own account of the team's fortunes.

He was by now stationed in Molesworth, England, and the life he describes seems a numbing routine of rain, mud, and fog interspersed with early morning takeoffs for bombing runs with frighteningly high casualty rates. Men died all around him, and in his telling of what took place in the skies over Europe, it seemed important that his father know his son's resolve and nerve never flagged. Within three months of arriving in England, half his unit was gone: "We still lack nose guns. The enemy is stronger and keener than ever and we don't miss a trip. Our effectiveness has been great. Our accuracy good. Courage and intestinal fortitude, as much as Napoleon or Washington might ask for." The waist gunner on his plane goes AWOL. The navigator is hospitalized. There is a raid on a submarine base in St. Nazaire. He gets

irritated describing commanders who are slow to pick up on his ideas. He goes to parties on leave in London. Missions are scrubbed at the last minute. Billy, Jr., kept a list of each of his missions, the position in which he flew, whether it was a win, and how significant the losses. He also wrote, "Little worried—Dad was sick at last writing and letter is overdue."

From time to time his picture appeared in the newspapers—gathered with his crew, joking with Bob Hope. He flew twenty-six missions and won the Distinguished Flying Cross and the Air Medal with three oak-leaf clusters. And then he came home.

"I never realized until he returned what tremendous pressure I was under," his father told Arthur Daley of the *New York Times*. "But now he's back home, safe at last."

Billy Southworth, Jr., was not going to become a major league baseball player. The airlines wanted him as a pilot. The movies wanted him, too. The producer Hunt Stromberg gave him a screen test and then signed him to a contract. His father seemed quite excited about this. But the war was not yet over, and so Billy, Jr., remained in uniform. The army sent him on tours to sell war bonds. Crowds of people came to see him. Enlisted men who accompanied him were grateful for his willingness to sneak them into officers' clubs. His future seemed one of endless possibilities. His father was regarded as one of the best managers in the game. And they were back together, at last. This is where the story should end.

But this is a wartime story, and such stories, even in a baseball context, too often end sadly. In February of 1945, Billy Southworth, Jr., who had managed to survive the hellishness of flak and German fighter planes over Europe, was killed on a routine training mission as he was about to land a B-29 at Mitchel Field, in New York. His father rushed to New York, and kept a vigil for weeks, waiting for his son's body to be recovered. It was not found until August.

Billy Southworth returned to Ohio, and then to the Cardinals, but he was never the same man again. Several years later he made a winner of the Boston Braves, but he had begun drinking again, and in time the Braves let him go. Years later he quit for good and ended his career as a scout. He died in 1969. He never saw the diary his son had written for him.

As it happened Billy, Jr.'s friend and navigator, Jon Schueler, had borrowed the diary. Schueler had dreams of becoming a writer and had asked Billy, Jr., if he might borrow the book to draw ideas and inspiration from it. Schueler, a sensitive man, had had a difficult time in the war, and saw in Billy, Jr.'s ease and bravery qualities he believed he himself lacked.

Schueler was also disposed to self-absorption, and so it never occurred to him to part with a diary whose front page bore a dedication to a man whose name was, after all, often in the news. Years later, Schueler did write about the war, and briefly about Billy, Jr., but mostly about his own life of struggle in a book called *The Sound of Sleat*. He also became an artist of some acclaim. His paintings, many of the sky, suggest a man searching for something in the clouds that had eluded him in wartime. Perhaps he was searching, too, in the words that Billy, Jr., had intended for another man, a baseball man, who would have surely understood his meaning.

Michael Shapiro is the author of five nonfiction books, most recently *The Last Good Season*. His work appears in such publications as the *New Yorker* and the *New York Times*. He is a professor of journalism at Columbia University and lives in New York with his wife and children.

THE BAT

Philip F. Deaver

Long before I knew how strangely literary the game is, I wrote and dreamed about baseball, because for me it's all tied up with memories and early initiations. A friend of mine who lived down the street when I was growing up was the son of a man who actually caught Warren Spahn, apparently during a lull in the action, at the Battle of the Bulge in World War II. As the story went, the mess sergeant provided this guy, who was a catcher back in the world, a slab of ham to put in his glove to take out a little of the bite while Spahnie aired out his heater to the delight of his war-weary pals. That catcher was the county surveyor in this story about the priest and the bat and the fly balls, the guy who allowed us to play baseball on the big green lawn of the Douglas County Court House in Tuscola, Illinois. I'd long wanted to write this piece as nonfiction, but it seemed so odd that our parish priest, the guy who hit me the pop-ups, was named Casey, really, and so there was this odd entanglement with the poem "Casey at the Bat." I call the priest Kelleher in my fiction, but I had to go with the truth here.

For perhaps ten years now the golden summer evenings I remember from growing up have been gone. Did they slip by and I didn't notice? And is it innocence or the light I'm missing? In my hometown in Illinois, the grass isn't as green as it was. When the rain comes, it comes in deluge and flood, or, for a long time, it doesn't come at all. In the 1950s, the winters were cold from well before Thanksgiving to well beyond April Fools' Day. Now the weather's a crapshoot.

The year I turned eleven, we ballplayers plunged into the summer as if it would be our last. We were bigger than the year before. Could greatness be far behind? We gathered in the mornings and played until about ten with an ash gray rubber-coated baseball, heavier than regulation, that gave off a smacking sound when you hit it. By ten the dew would have burned off and from then on we used a regular ball. There was a park on the north side of town where we played, and on the south side, where I lived, there were a couple of insufficient lots we managed to play in sometimes if nothing was shaking out at the park. Frequently, we used the southwest corner of the block occupied by the Douglas County Court House, a huge expanse of green. Home plate was under a giant silver maple, and third was a sugar maple lightning-damaged into a strange shape and much smaller than the silver. We'd use the batting team's ball gloves as first and second bases. Rightfield was closed because of the courthouse itself and two stalwart limestone boulders chiseled to make a stand to display a Civil War cannon, the cannon long-since gone, so we didn't encourage the participation of lefthanded hitters (there weren't many anyway), and left-center was very deep, if you got the ball high in the air early enough so it didn't tangle in the rangy green limbs of third base. The courthouse venue was far from perfect, but the grass was cool and always mowed, and in afternoon sun, the shade was worth the trouble of the trees.

The courthouse was two blocks from my home. The summer we were mostly eleven but turning twelve was the only summer we played there.

You have to picture this. There wasn't really a diamond; we made it all up. There was no backstop, and the batting team supplied both the pitcher and the catcher. If the ball went between the catcher's legs, it skipped a few times and went across Van Allen Street right into the front yard of the Forty Martyrs Catholic Church and rectory.

In those golden evenings that year, Father James Casey, our pastor, would walk at a peculiarly fast pace up and down the sidewalks around his house, saying his office. He'd been injured a few months before in a one-person car wreck returning to town from the Kaskaskia Golf Course, and the walking had been prescribed as a way of rehabbing his hurt leg. Father Casey, first-generation Irishman, was a helluva golfer. It amazes me to calculate that at the time I'm talking about he was younger than I am now as I sit here writing about him. He was in his mid-fifties, and was an institution in our town, having been in Tuscola for twenty-five years. Among the Protestant townsfolk, he was known as tough, perhaps a little cranky and mysterious. In fact, my Catholic classmates saw him that way, too. He barked at us in catechism classes, in a brogue so thick we couldn't understand him. He was a great friend of my dad, though, and frequently came to our house for Sunday dinner, so I did "get" this fellow a bit better than my friends did. Anyway, to a man, the kids I played ball with were afraid of him, and if the ball went across the street when Father Casey was out in his yard, I was the one who had to go after it.

One evening, I'm sure it was a Wednesday, I trotted over to the courthouse after dinner to meet my friends—you only needed about six to have a good game—and sat under the silver maple waiting for them to show up. Andy would soon round the corner on Houghton (that was centerfield on the courthouse diamond), Gary would come down from the north side via Court Street, and Alan would come on Central up from where his folks had an apartment on the highway. Bill would show up probably, and maybe bring a brother, hopefully not the littlest one. I waited. It was never perfect. We never got the time of the rendezvous quite right, and unexpected circumstances would always arise. (Bill's folks might load up the family and go out to the drive-in if there was a good Western showing; Gary's dad might make him work.)

I waited for them. I was used to it—in fact we all were. They waited for me plenty, too, in those days. We were eleven and flexible. Sometimes nothing happened, and whoever was waiting would finally walk home kicking a rock. That evening, though, Casey was fast-walking and reading his breviary, and I sat under the tree so that I wasn't completely visible to him, so he wouldn't call me over to talk. I hated to stand around and talk to adults. "How's your dad?" "How's your mom?" "When you gonna learn your Latin responses so you can serve mass?" "How's school?"

I knew he knew I was sitting under the maple, but if I was on the other side of the tree, that seemed to let us both off the hook. He wouldn't have to talk nice to me just because he was pals with my dad and knew me and came to dinner sometimes. And I wouldn't have to talk to him a whole lot so next time he'd recognize my voice in the confessional, which was precisely the sort of thing an eleven-year-old boy worried about if the family was friends with the priest and the boy was me.

So, on this evening apparently none of my friends were coming, and after a while, when his walk got him directly across the street from me, he called over. His voice came around the tree.

"Danny. You over there?"

Because my father and I had the same name, my nickname was Danny in those days, after the Kipling poem "They're Hanging Danny Deever in the Morning." Things like that can affect your destiny.

"Want me to hit you some?" he called to me.

Right, I was thinking. Hundred-year-old Irish priest—a golfer—with a broken leg—is gonna hit me some. Plus, my Protestant pals start filtering in from the neighborhood and see the priest duffing around with our ball bat, they'd just go back home. "That's it," they'd be thinking. "No baseball tonight!"

"Sure," I said.

He looked both ways on Van Allen, limped across the street. He gimped up to me, and I got up off the ground where I'd been sitting.

"How's your dad?" he asked.

"Fine."

"Fine what?"

"Fine, Father."

"Lemme see that thing," he said, and I got him my bat, which was lean-ing against the tree. It was a twenty-nine-inch Larry Doby Louisville Slugger. I always brought it to our games. Bill had a thirty-inch Hank Aaron we all used, and Andy had a thirty-two-inch Jackie Robinson we'd broken sometime in the past year but still used after it was repaired, using a well-placed nail to hold it together plus two miles of electrical tape around the handle and over the nail, which effectively removed the nail from our consciousness. (After it broke, this repaired bat logged most of our tape-measure home runs, and we had a theory that the nail and the tape were responsible. It didn't occur to us we were growing.) Anyway, Father Casey handled my Larry Doby like it was a foreign object.

"Where's the ball?" he said, and I took it out of my glove over by the tree. He handled it a minute. It was the rubber-coated one. We often used it at the courthouse because the leather ones got torn up on the sidewalk and the street. All it took to tear the thread was for the ball to skip once on the concrete—one little tear in the thread and a leather baseball was on borrowed time.

Father Casey, wearing black pants and a white shirt with rolled-up sleeves and a Roman collar, scanned the big west lawn of the courthouse. That's how it would have looked to him—a big lawn. He couldn't see the baseball diamond so clearly imagined by us kids. He said, "Okay, I'll go over there by the steps and then hit 'em this way so we miss the trees."

"Yes, Father," I said.

As he lumbered away, he said, over his shoulder, "How's your mom?" "Good."

"Good what?"

"Good, Father."

I watched him as he slowly strolled through the courthouse lawn's green grass until he was right up to the building itself, right under the window of the county surveyor (Bill's dad). I watched him go, on his sore leg, sort of slumped like the ancient guy he was. This would never work. Golf and baseball aren't the same. If you didn't know that already, you could tell by the way he handled bat and ball as he walked. I looked around for the approach of my friends from their dinners. Nobody was coming. Okay.

I guessed trying to hit a baseball to some kid was the sort of thing that would make Father feel better. Step across the street and hit some balls, try out the mending leg in something besides walking around the house two hundred times. He put his black breviary on one of the courthouse steps and pushed up his already rolled sleeves. He looked down the long lawn my way like he was scoping out a tee shot, took a couple of practice swings, very golfish. This would never work. Then he took the ball and laid it out in front of himself on the evening air, and quickly brought his hand back to the bat handle so both hands were on it . . .

. . . and smacked the mightiest fly ball almost straight up that I had ever seen hit by priest, man, or real baseball player, straight up damned near out of sight . . .

. . . and yelled to me as it went up, "HaHA! Catch that one, Danny boy!"

Well, it turns out golf is not baseball but when it comes to hitting, the two sports do have some things in common. We who grew up hitting a baseball (and, since, have played a little golf) have learned to dream of hitting one that would fly like a shot off the tee, launched effortlessly, rocketing away in a white streak breathtaking in the beauty of its flight against the background of trees and green grass, taking to the air in an upward swoop that would make the best-hit line drive into the gap seem lumbering by comparison. It turns out Father Casey could whack some mighty fly balls.

There were many evenings after that when I chased pop-ups at the courthouse. Casey, grumbly old parish priest, seemed to love coming over and hitting, and I loved trying to track those giants down. It was fun despite the obstacles: the trees, the cannon rocks, the crisscross of sidewalks, and telephone wires. I imagined sometime getting him to hit flies to me at the Pony League field in the park, but this wasn't that kind of thing. We were stuck in the circumstances of sandlot baseball contrived within available space convenient to Father Casey if he wanted to wander across the street on a summer afternoon. It was a situation confined to a certain situation. One night toward the end of summer as I watched him launch me pop-ups, I finally noticed something I hadn't before. The ball wasn't being pitched to him; rather, he was tossing it up and hitting it by himself. Now I noticed he was tucking a shoulder and shortening the stroke. Many times he was fouling the ball off, though they were mighty fouls to be sure, and sometimes you could tell even when he hit it on the sweet spot he didn't get it all. And I thought to myself:

If only. He had. A better bat.

In those days, an eleven-year-old could spot a good bat. Even the sandlot kids could eye the ash or hickory and see promise in the grain of the wood, tell what felt right in the distribution of the weight between the handle and the barrel. They could take a couple of practice swings and know if it was good in the hands. It was intuition and experience, not science; it was also partly faith. If the bat felt right, so did the batter when he stepped to the plate.

The Saturday morning after my birthday—twelve!—I had a little birthday cash. I biked uptown seven blocks to the Western Auto, where I found Father Casey a thin-handled hickory beauty: a thirty-four-inch Mickey Mantle Louisville Slugger, beautiful, the wood a dark tan, browned in fire with a varnish. *Powerized*, it said on the bat above the label in parentheses shaped like lightning. The grain was very interesting. The lines that ran the length of the bat were distinct and spaced, and the wood was harder and sweeter than the thin-grained cheapos we had in Little League.

It was four years before Mantle and Maris, using this new bat style, made a run at Babe Ruth's single-season home-run record. The older bat style was thick and heavy; old-timers often said people should remember Babe Ruth set that famous record basically hitting a sock with a fence post. The Mickey Mantle model was thin-handled, the barrel, too, thinner than you'd expect. The knob on the end of it was pronounced so it didn't slip out of the hitter's hand. Think about a golf club, the metal shaft light, with plenty of whip. And of course the golf ball was packed with rubber bands instead of yarn. Yarn! Anyway, I imagined this was the kind of bat Father Cascy needed if he was going to take his talent for hitting fly balls to the next level. Light, the sweet spot farther away from him for whip action and so he wouldn't have to tuck in his shoulders as he turned but rather could extend his arms, the handle so he could grip it tight and transfer arm speed and shoulder ballast directly into pop.

"Where'd this come from?" he asked me that first evening.

"Try it," I said.

He started meandering up the lawn toward the courthouse to his usual spot. "It looks brand-new. Did I break the other one?"

"Nah, it's at home."

"Uh-huh." He was standing up there by the steps taking practice swings. "I might knock somebody's window out with this thing."

"Yes, Father," I said.

I wanted all the fly ball this man could whack into the sky.

That evening some of my Protestant friends showed up and watched him hit—the mysterious local Catholic priest hitting pop flies at the courthouse. Only in America.

And what a thrill it was, the crack of that new bat, how the ball sailed above the full length of the courthouse lawn, high over the silver maple and the little dwarf maple we called third base, passed over Central Street like a Russian satellite a couple of years later, flew over Charlie Price's garden in the next block and a yard beyond that, so high it was nearly out of sight in the pink dusky sky of a rural Illinois evening, summer 1957. I ran back for it, across Central and down the alley. I ran for it as far as I could go, right up against Judge Gray's handsome wrought iron fence. Lined up in windows behind Father Casey, the county surveyor and his staff looked on. Across the street to the south on the curb in front of the Catholic church, friends saw it happen and would testify.

"Yikes," my friend Andy said without really knowing he said it, sitting by the silver maple looking up. The ball, as it returned to earth, seemed to fall straight down out of the pink and blue, straight into Judge Gray's wife's flower garden, and didn't even bounce in the loam.

"Yikes indeed, lad!" Father Casey called. "Ha HAA!" he laughed. I'd never seen him happy like that. "Now that's a ball bat!" he said so we coulhear him and he laughed again. I can hear him this moment. Will you cry with me right now for the loss of that innocent, beautiful time?

Philip F. Deaver is the thirteenth winner of the Flannery O'Connor Award. He has held fellowships from the National Endowment for the Arts and Bread Loaf. His short fiction has appeared in *Prize Stories: The O. Henry Awards* and has been recognized in *Best American Short Stories* and *The Pushcart Prize.* His poems are collected in *How Men Pray* (Anhinga Press). In recent years, he has also published memoir and creative nonfiction in the literary magazines and edited a book of creative nonfiction essays on baseball, entitled *Scoring from Second: Writers on Baseball* (University of Nebraska Press). He is a professor of English and permanent writer-inresidence at Rollins College, Winter Park, Florida, and teaches on the fiction faculty in the Spalding University brief residency MFA program in Louisville, Kentucky.

MY OUTFIELD

J. D. Scrimgeour

Winner of the *Creative Nonfiction* Baseball Essay Contest

This essay originated from my experiences playing the outfield. From Little League through high school, my outfields rarely involved fences. Somewhere far behind me would be a cornfield, or a softball diamond, or just grass. Where did the game end and the world—or imagination—begin?

The outfield stretches from the flat, dried brown grass of Fairview Park in Normal, Illinois, to the thick green behind the high school tennis courts in New Milford, Connecticut, to Furlong Field in Salem, Massachusetts, booby-trapped with gooseshit, hemmed in on three sides by an auto junkyard, a playground, and a street, but on its fourth side—is that fair territory?—sloping down into the mouth of the North River as it drifts into the Atlantic.

Its boundaries are inexact, and infinite—a state of mind.

It's a dumping ground for the weak-armed, the unskilled, the lefthanded; its grasses are littered with failures. Even Whitman, the supreme outfielder (unshaven, musing, great range), would be perplexed by grass so full of misjudgments.

The outfield is tainted with mercury and lead paint; it's an old Indian burial ground. Ambiguous weeds make love to lost strands of grass in the shadow of an imaginary scoreboard. The brown patches where the outfielders usually stand weep like bullet holes. A hollow, anonymous voice slurs facts that pile in soggy heaps down the leftfield line. Where the grass turns to yellow stalks of prairie, an ant skitters into the husk of a baseball, empty leather hide that has birthed whatever was inside it.

There are no fathers and sons in the outfield. There is, somehow, not enough room. Beyond the foul lines, there have been sightings of gnarled gods with curious, knobby protrusions and unpronounceable names—the sentimental call them angels.

The low line drive skims the infield and bounds toward you, a little to your right. Nobody on, one out. You need simply to stop the ball. The throw, which needn't be rushed, will go to the shortstop, who is lining himself up with second base. The ball is still moving fast, but it's on the ground. Plant one knee in the grass, the other bent, leg opening out. The glove touches the ground, your throwing hand beside it, fingers splayed. Watch the ball into the glove, closing your hand over it, getting hold of it as you push yourself up, angling your body in line with second. The arm drops and rises behind you, your glove points to your target, then falls as you shift your weight and release. Whooshhhhhh—snap! into the shortstop's mitt. The shortstop turns and jogs the few steps to the infield dirt, watching the runner retreat to first, then flips the ball to the pitcher. Single.

Mostly, the outfielder runs to back up, to collect a poor throw, or a surprising bounce, to limit others' mistakes, to assure everyone that things are not *that* bad. Hustle behind third base. Be ready for the pickoff to second, the overthrow from third to first. Mostly—and ideally—these efforts are unrewarded. The play is made, the outfielder jogs back to his post, glove unused, breath easing to normal, perhaps hollering "Good play" or "Way to do it" as he folds into position, knees bent, hand on one knee and glove on the other. Settled, he spits, as if saying, *That's done.*

If things go perfectly, the pitcher never lets the ball leave the infield. Logically, the outfielder's ideal game is one in which he does nothing. There he is, scuffing the grass with his cleat, spitting sunflower seeds, offering some bland encouragement that the pitcher may not even hear. There he is, lying down and staring up at the empty, endless sky, the greatest outfield, uncoverable. He plucks a blade of grass and pins it between his teeth. A plane leaves a contrail that connects one cloud to another. It is just cool enough that when a breeze passes, goose bumps appear on his arms.

The outfield, even centerfield, is not for strivers, those cursed with ambition or pride. Lear ends up in the outfield, raging in a storm (why didn't they call the game?), but he never imagined he would be out there, rain spilling from his cap's brim.

The outfield is democratic. Anyone can play it, and, let's admit, any number can play it. Twelve players on your T-ball team? Have six outfielders.

This country, drifting toward empire, more proud than democratic, has little interest in the outfield. In the major leagues, the fences keep getting closer and closer. The possibilities, the players, must be hemmed in.

Watch an infielder groom his position, bending every now and then to pick up a small rock and toss it beyond the baseline, out of play. Such fastidiousness! Obsessive-compulsive, clean-shaven or finely mustachioed, they are too tidy. *Are my pants too loose? My socks the right height? Is my cap precisely centered and angled off the forehead?*

What can an outfielder do? The task is Sisyphean. One can't tidy the universe. Pick up a rock or dirt clod and move it . . . where? And what about the other rocks, pebbles, twigs? The logs and memories and boulders? A ball could go anywhere. One must resign oneself to fate—the ball will collide with what it chooses. The world will go where it goes. You are not central to its outcome. The bombs will fall, and you can do little to stop them. Back up! Always back up! Or, if the situation calls for it, run like hell, holding your glove ahead of you like an offering, or a prayer.

In a time of war, the outfield may be your only chance.

Don't believe them when they tell you all fields have fences now. Don't even believe them when you see the fences yourself, when you collide into them running back, back, back for that endless fly ball. There is always more air than chain-link, and some nocturnal animal will have dug a rut underneath. There must be a way out.

• • •

An inside pitch, and eight-year-old Javier drops the bat and jumps back, out of the box, pulling his chest in, his arms rising on either side like wings. He turns to his bench wide-eyed. "That ball almost hit me!" he exclaims, not with anger, or fear, but with simple astonishment that the world has the potential for such cruelty. The coach simply nods.

Oh Javier, there is room for you in the outfield. You don't need to wear cleats. You don't need to wear sneakers—go barefoot. You can forget your hat in your mother's boyfriend's car. You can forget to pee between innings, and then, in the privacy of rightfield, drop your gray baseball pants down to your thighs in full view of those parents in the stands, of your own teammates on the bench, of your coach. Your only audience is yourself. You had to go bad, and now you're going, the stream making an impressive arc, leaping into the air like a well-struck ball. A few drops glisten on the grass, rivulets putter and fade into the earth, a map of some unknown country appears and quickly recedes.

• • •

Turn to the rightfielder, the young guy who is supposed to be good, the one who aches for your position, and yell "Kevin!" When he turns, open and close your mouth as if you are talking, but, rather than say words, just let out occasional syllables—"Ah-Bo-Ace-Ta-Ta-Jedda." Smile as if you've said something clever. Watch him smile, nod, and offer a weak laugh. What pleasure to be goofy! He thinks you're annoying, or nuts. He's certain you're not as good as he is (he belongs in the infield). Lift your cap off your head, rub your long hair off your brow with your arm, then get ready for the pitch.

In the outfield, I smoked pot. I cracked stupid jokes about sex I only half understood. I rode in cars, their tires cutting the turf, making ridges in the moonlight. I stood in line, waiting for my turn, for the coach to hit me ten fly balls in a row until my arm burned from all those throws back in, until my lungs burned from all that running. In the outfield, I composed the great song of the spheres I will never sing aloud, that I have half forgotten now, as I enter middle age.

In the outfield, worms eased between the nubs of my cleats, trying to write their damp hieroglyphics on my soles.

Yes, we were naked in the outfield, and I can hardly remember her now, but it was good.

In the silences of centerfield, I etched haikus on the back of my glove:

I was of three minds,

like an outfield, in which there are three outfielders.

From a distance, the outfielder stands, small and thin, a young boy's erect penis, so insignificant on the huge body of the field. Something passing over him that is

vague, unknown, presexual, keeps him from dropping limp on the grass. The breeze? The clouds? Whitman's trembling hand? The pitch?

The outfielder's pleasure is simple, unencumbered by guilt or desire: See ball. Chase ball. Get ball. Throw ball. Oh, joy!

The outfielder does not wear a protective cup. He does not speak of fences.

• • •

You have taken turns on the pitcher's mound and spent a little glamour time at shortstop, but you have always been an outfielder. When you were nine, playing in a league of nine- and ten-year-olds, you were the worst hitter on a first-place team. You spent that season excited and terrified, standing on the fringes of the outfield. Kids rarely hit the ball farther than the edge of the infield dirt. One game, the main slugger on the other team, a kid named Todd Whitehouse, hit a monstrous fly ball out toward you. You watched it. You stepped toward it. You caught it. And you were baptized an outfielder, teammates slapping your back and hollering. Since then, you've believed you can catch any ball you can reach, and many you can't.

And to throw! Not like infielders, the wrist snap and quick release. Outfielders throw with their lungs, their soul, their groin. The body flings itself open, as if to hug the world, one arm somewhere behind the back, the other hanging in front, and then the swift arc of the body and arm, nearly a somersault, and the ball zings off.

A secret: true outfielders—not those who toil in the major leagues— abhor hitting. To be the spectacle—how distressingly public. And it's so violent, brutal. Batting is something the outfielder accepts, penance for the joy of hunting fly balls, a kind of tax.

It is hardly worth running hard if you don't get to dive, stretching parallel to the ground and falling into it at the end. The batter begins to swing, and before he even hits the ball, you're taking a step left or right, depending on the pitch location and the speed of the swing. The ball moves up and out, and you are moving, too, your body calculating geometry on the run—the best angle, the quickest route, exactly where the little fucker is going. You're running so hard you forget you're running, and you lose all the awkward hitches that make you slower than you should be. Whisk, whisk, across the grass, whisk, whisk. And the ball comes down, and your body calculates again—is a dive necessary? If so, how? What angle? Off which leg?

Now! The arm stretches. . . . Snap! Thud! It's in the glove. You're on the ground. You hop up and hurl the ball back to the infield, back from whence it came, and feel your chest rise and fall, rise and fall. When you lie down tonight, your side will be tender, and you will be unable to sleep, your chest still rising and falling, your mind chasing that ball down in the great dark field of night.

J. D. Scrimgeour's book _Themes for English B: A Professor's Education In and Out of Class_ won the AWP Award for Creative Nonfiction in 2005 and was published by the University of Georgia Press in 2006. He is also the author of another book of nonfiction, _Spin Moves_, and a collection of poetry, _The Last Miles._ His essays have appeared in several venues, including the _Boston Globe Magazine_ and _The Chronicle of Higher Education._ He is coordinator of creative writing at Salem State College in Salem, Massachusetts, and the assistant coach on his sons' baseball team.

ORIOLE MAGIC

Elizabeth Bobrick

Writing "Oriole Magic" was full of surprises for me. I'd never written about sports, and until Lee Gutkind asked me for an essay for this collection, I didn't know I had this story in me, or how well I remembered the baseball columns I'd first read so long ago. Above all, writing this essay allowed me to be amazed once again by the miracle of reading and writing: that, somehow, we are able to grasp the slender threads made of words and fashion them into lifelines.

This is a happy story about becoming a fan, although it began unhappily for me, and ended unhappily for my heroes.

When I fell for the Baltimore Orioles in the summer of 1979, I was a twenty-three-year-old graduate student. The Birds and I were about the same age, give or take a few years. I, however, lived in books, largely indoors, and almost entirely on nerve; they, in the words of sportswriter Dan Okrent, spent their youth and energy "attempting to touch their feet safely on a pentagonal piece of rubber more times than their opponents."[1]

I'd moved to Baltimore to enter a Ph.D. program in Classics, the study of ancient Greek and Roman culture. From the age of twelve, I had planned to become a professor and stay in school forever. The track of my existence was a narrow one: from my desk at home, to my desk in the basement of the library, to my desk in class, and then back to the library, and eventually back to my desk at home.

Still, there was no way for a sentient, even marginally socialized adult living in Baltimore to remain unaware of the town's beloved O's. That summer, they were winning like crazy and pulling in record-breaking crowds. I lived not far from Memorial Stadium, close enough to see the klieg lights in the night sky from my bedroom window. But it never occurred to me to actually go watch a game. It wasn't that I considered baseball beneath me. I just didn't do sports. I did school.

• • •

Recalling graduate school, for me, is like recalling childbirth or the experience of passing a kidney stone: I can no longer feel what I felt at the time, but I remember it felt very bad. Although I loved Sophocles, Plato, Homer, Virgil, the philosophers, and the historians, I did not love the endless hours of largely solitary work. From nine in the morning until midnight almost every day, I struggled to read the surviving literary masterpieces in their original languages. And literature was only part of what we needed to know: there were the vases, columns, and statuary of two cultures; their wars, laws, and class struggles; dialects, corrupted texts, and the reconstructed protolanguage from which Greek and Latin are said to be descended. I took four classes a semester and wrote long research papers for each.

In my second year, 1979, I did all this and taught a class of my own three times a week, to forty undergraduates all roughly my age, with no guidance from anyone, and without much success. That is to say, I bombed. The kindest of my student evaluations was this: "Ms. Bobrick would be a good teacher if she would prepare."

The only good thing about my lack of training and supervision was that, except for my unlucky charges, I had no witnesses. Except for teaching, everything we graduate students did was a performance for our professors, an attempt to show them how much we knew, how hard we worked, how brilliant and original were our ideas. These men—and they were all men—served as our profession's umpires, coaches, and scouts. Some were kind, some were not, but at any moment, any of them could decide to withdraw his support, and if that happened, there was no court of appeal. My fellow students and I did our best to act as a team: we studied together, complained together, encouraged each other, and threw noisy parties. But we were competing with each other, not just for approval, but, eventually, for real jobs in the big world.

● ● ●

That was school. Not-school was worse.

Straight out of college, and against my parents' wishes, I'd married a brilliant and charismatic but only sporadically employed academic who treated me as if I were a freshman in his first-year philosophy seminar. I didn't think to object; I had allotted myself only one identity, that of a student. From one month to the next, my husband and I walked a tightrope of part-time jobs, short-term grants, and high-interest credit. He settled his nerves with expensive aged bourbon, to the extent that our monthly tab at the neighborhood liquor store began to exceed our utility bills. I became expert at begging for a little more time from the nice ladies at C & P phone company and Baltimore Gas and Electric.

All right, big deal, I was young and strong—except for one thing. Immediately prior to my first year of graduate school, I was diagnosed with epilepsy. The humiliating grand mal seizures could be controlled by medication, but they felt like monsters at my core, straining at their chains. I was afraid above all that I would have one in class, and the illness reduced my already constrained freedoms: I wasn't supposed to drink or drive or get too tired (right) or even too emotional.

My New Year's resolution during these years was always to stop worrying, but I never had any success. Too nervous to eat, I lost twenty pounds during my first semester. I didn't feel sorry for myself (although I admit that I rather do now, looking back), or wonder if this was a good way to live. As silly as it seems, I saw my life as a heroic struggle. For the heroes of ancient epic and tragedy, struggle lent dignity to the mess of human life. Struggle purified a bad situation. Like Oedipus, I was flawed, but my goal, to find truth and self-knowledge, was noble. Like Odysseus, I trusted in my wits to somehow get me out of this mess. Like an idiot, I thought being unhappy would ultimately make me a better person.

Enter the Orioles, by way of what Homer called "winged words."

• • •

When I wasn't strong-arming my fears, my perceived failings, or my actual folly; when I wasn't hacking at Aeschylus's thorn-thicket vocabulary, or Thucydides's head-bangingly hard syntax, I tried to relax. I listened to classical music, I read fiction, but mostly I read the papers—read the print off them. We didn't have a television—too tempting a distraction from work—so the papers were my one connection to the world outside school. Mine were the *Baltimore Evening Sun,* soon to be absorbed into what was then the *Morning Sun,* and the great *Washington Star,* now gone for twenty-five years. When I had time, I read the *Washington Post* as well. I read every section—except the sports pages.

The best thing about reading the paper was that it allowed me to procrastinate. Unlike daydreaming about what I would do if I were suddenly, tragically, widowed, and how I would then decorate my single-girl apartment, reading the paper was a justifiable use of time—no less than a citizen's duty.

One beautiful evening in June of 1979, my desire to forestall four more hours at my desk was so strong that I picked up the sports section of the *Evening Sun*. On its front page was an article by someone named Terry Pluto. I laughed, thinking not of Disney's dog, but of the Greek god of wealth and the underworld, the god who had pulled the shrieking Persephone underground to be his queen.

I learned from Pluto that 1970 had been the last year the Orioles had a championship season, and that their play had been haphazard since then. But this year, apparently, looked promising. The O's had snapped awake from their slumbers. They were riding a winning streak, reminding everyone of what they used to be and raising hopes for another spell of glory.

Pluto had devoted this column to somebody named Jim Palmer, a pitcher from the former dynasty, and the only member of the team who was nationally recognized as a star. Palmer, I read, had a chronic problem. He felt unappreciated by his manager, a dyspeptic little man named Earl Weaver. Palmer was given to sulking and saying his arm hurt, when in fact it was his ego that was sore, because Weaver didn't let him pitch as often as he wanted to. As Pluto reported, Palmer was threatening to aggravate management until they got so sick of him that they traded him.[2]

I liked this Palmer: handsome, accomplished, angry, no false modesty. A modern-day Achilles, I thought, a skillful warrior, sick of being bossed around by someone far inferior. No one in Homer's original audience would have had any trouble understanding Palmer's grievance.

The hardworking Pluto had a second piece in the paper that day, this one about the Orioles' recent road trip to Cleveland. A rainstorm had forced the game to be called, and a melee ensued, during which the home fans tore up the stadium while being chased through mud by the police. Both constabulary and quarry slipped and fell a good deal. Pluto said the scene, one "worthy of the Keystone Kops," played out against a dramatic backdrop: "The sky was filled with lightning. The rain came down in torrents and Noah could be heard in the background pounding the last few nails into his ark."[3]

I had never seen reporting like this: a description of the weather apparently lifted from a Gothic novel followed by an allusion to the Book of Genesis, all in order to

take a swipe at the Cleveland fans' wild behavior and their police force's ineptitude. I admired the boldness of the mix, and the broad brushstroke delivery.

It seemed the players could sling words, too. Pluto concluded by quoting Orioles outfielder John Lowenstein's analysis of the evening: "I'd say that 65 percent of the people living in Cleveland are manic depressives and the game is just an excuse to blow their minds out."[4] Such a statement elsewhere in the paper would have to be balanced by an outraged denial from the mayor of Cleveland. Not in the sports pages, apparently, where the reporters enjoyed true freedom of the press.

I opened the paper a few days later to find the following by guest columnist Edwin Pope of the *Miami Herald,* who contrasted the workmanlike,

unified Orioles to the louder, less cohesive Yankees: "Some who find this type hard to read will remember when the Yankees were merely a baseball team. Now they are a morality play. Except with these hams, it is difficult to tell the heroes from the villains. . . . Jean-Paul Sartre couldn't have been talking about baseball when he said, 'Words are loaded pistols.' Else there wouldn't be a Yankee alive."[5]

Morality plays? Sartre? In the sports section? How had I not known about this kind of writing—or the appeal of the Birds themselves? They were such an engaging cast of characters. Weaver tore up rulebooks on the field to illustrate for the umpires their willful disregard for the game. He was constantly ejected from the game by these same men, which was in fact his goal, the better to interrupt the other team's momentum. John Lowenstein was articulate, intelligent, and endowed with a strong sense of the absurd. Rick Dempsey, the catcher, led the fans in cheers and entertained them with a vaudeville-style pantomime during rain delays. Doug DeCinces, the third baseman, muscled and mustachioed, looked as if he had stepped out of a team photo from 1897. Outfielder Ken Singleton was mighty at bat, modest and team-minded with reporters, and as serenely handsome as Apollo. The denizens of the bull pen, including Cy Young-winner Palmer, had skill and enough quirky personality to put on a show of their own.

But none of the Birds impressed me so much as first baseman and switch-hitter Eddie Murray. With the intuitive grasp of an idiot savant, I was drawn to this future Hall of Famer, a poker-faced man with the wide brown eyes of a boy. I knew from my reading that he was quick as a muscle twitch in the infield, and famously laconic in the presence of reporters. (*Evening Sun* columnist Kevin Cowherd was later to describe him as someone who "tossed around words like they were $100 bills.")[6] He was my favorite from the start. As I followed the team more intently, something mysterious happened, something that seems unbelievable to me now—even a little nuts. I began to take on the players as role models. They seemed to have exactly the strengths that I lacked, and I was desperate for inspiration and a sense of belonging. The men I read about in the papers somehow provided me with both. What I knew of them through the written word—ever my guide to life—was enough to change my idea of heroism, and of myself. The advertising jingle for the Birds consisted of five words, repeated over and over: "Oriole Magic—Make It Happen." I fell under the sway of that magic.

The team gave me a new way to think about struggle. So I had epilepsy. Did that have to mean I was an invalid, someone who couldn't do this and couldn't do that? Hell no. I was doing as much as anybody, and *I was playing hurt*, something all the best guys did, because you do what you set out to do. When a professor was harshly critical of a paper I'd been proud of, I saw it as a temporary setback rather than proof that I was no good at this and never would be. All I had to do was *stick it out until I broke my losing streak* and *come back all the stronger*, which I did. It was okay to have fears; the Birds weren't fearless. Gary Roenicke, who had been knocked down by a pitch to the face, wasn't ashamed to admit how much he didn't want to get hit again. He wore a custom-made batting helmet with a face mask. "Baseball is a game of survival," he said, "not macho."[7] So I didn't have to deny my fears, either— just face them, and maybe take a little more joy in my work, as the O's did in theirs.

By August, with the pennant race heating up, the masters of sports-writing weighed in. I read my first Red Smith column that October, when the Birds battled the California Angels. Smith took his inspiration from that team's heavenly name:

[Lowenstein] was elected to sainthood by acclamation when he reached out and sliced one of John Montague's forkballs into the seats just inside the foul pole, and 52,108 worshippers cemented his place in the celestial hierarchy the first time he went to bat in the second game yesterday. . . . Pope John Paul II has not received a more reverent reception in Ireland or the United States than parishioners in Memorial Stadium gave their newly minted godling . . . not even two strikeouts and an infield grounder stilled the cries of his idolators.[8]

I remember looking up "godling" to make sure he had not invented the word. Then there was Tom Callahan of the *Washington Star,* whose sentence structure reminded me of Cicero's. When the Orioles were one game away from winning the Series, he wrote: "Earl Weaver loudly says *he* is to be the star of the Baltimore Orioles, a plain fact that amuses the players at the brink of the World Championship; which annoys them occasionally; which hurts their feelings frequently; which helped them to the brink of the championship undeniably."[9] Behold, a one-sentence illustration of what adverbs can do when a professional strikes the keys. (The Orioles ended up losing the World Series to the Pittsburgh Pirates, but you would never have known it in Baltimore, or by me.)

At the end of that season, John Lowenstein said something that affected me like nothing else I had read since June. Turning serious, for once, he told Terry Pluto, "People ask if I was afraid that I might do something stupid on national TV, like fall down under a fly ball. That never enters a ballplayer's mind. No one reaches the majors with that type of negative thinking and plays with the fear of embarrassing themselves in the back of their minds."[10] When I read this, I knew I had received my marching orders. If I was going to reach the majors, I had to start trusting myself. My customary toxic, corroding worry was not going to help me. This was news.

● ● ●

By opening day of the 1980 season, I could recite Earl Weaver's exquisitely machined starting lineup (Palmer, Dempsey, Dauer, DeCinces, Murray, Bumbry, Roenicke, Singleton, and Belanger and Garcia, who took turns at shortstop). I knew the names and faces of his "deep depth" pitching staff (McGregor, Palmer, Flanagan, Stone, Stewart, and an infantry of daredevil relievers). Eddie had become the mentor of a new kid, Cal Ripken, Jr., known to fans as "Little Rip," in deference to his revered father, Cal, Sr., third-base coach and an Orioles veteran. But I'd still never seen a game at the stadium.

I'd been afraid of crowds since my seizures began. After watching the 1979 Series on a borrowed twelve-inch black-and-white TV, however, I thought I might risk it. I walked to Memorial Stadium with some friends. I sipped at forbidden tubs of National Bohemian beer and did not mention that I hated the official song for the

seventh-inning stretch, John Denver's "Thank God I'm a Country Boy." In other words, I became a regular fan, watching a game that was no longer confined to my imagination, and sharing its pleasures with my fellow citizens.

The Birds held steady for three seasons—1980, 1981, 1982—not making it into the playoffs, but holding second place in their division. That was good enough for me (and the rest of Baltimore). I loved my Birds, I knew them better than ever, and I had faith in them, just as I had more and more faith in myself. My Greek, my Latin, and my teaching were all so much improved that school was almost—almost—a pleasure.

But the summer of 1983 put both the Orioles and me to the test. I was cramming for my last set of exams before the dissertation, the comprehensives, or "comps," as they are known. If I didn't do well on these hours-long tests, my years of graduate school would get me nothing more than "the terminal M.A.," the consolation prize for getting kicked out of the Ph.D. program. The Birds, meanwhile, were in disarray. Key players were injured or suffering from personal problems that translated into slumps. Palmer had been sent down to the farm team to brush up on his humility (officially, to recover from an injury). The pundits were pessimistic.

Then, in August, the O's were suddenly themselves again. All at once their enemies fell before them. The Birds silenced the bats and the mouths of the hated Yankees. Then they pulled down the White Sox in the playoffs, and sailed into the Series, as they last had in 1979, again vying with a team from Pennsylvania: not the Pittsburgh Pirates this time, but the Philadelphia Phillies.

The Orioles were proud to be winning, and prouder of having maintained their focus and friendship in the bad times. But still they did not brag about themselves or sneer at others—at a time when Reggie Jackson had made those dugout diversions into an art form. Nor did they shoulder each other aside for attention. Older players mentored younger ones. Their code of conduct, supported by the new manager, Joe Altobelli, was known as the Oriole Way, and it set them apart from other ball clubs.

So as the O's entered the Series, all was well once again, except for one player: my beloved Eddie Murray. Still mired in his season-long slump, he was consistent only in making completely uncharacteristic errors.

His performance in the Series was equally dismal—until the final game, when he scored a base hit and two back-to-back homers. Then, as Kevin Cowherd of the *Evening Sun* wrote, "With three swings of a bat on a crisp autumn evening, Eddie Murray had ripped the throat out of his slump, ripped a hole in the thinking that says he cannot hit in the pressure games."[11] We were redeemed—and I passed my comps.

• • •

Unexpectedly and unaccountably, the Orioles fell apart after they won the Series. The spirit seemed to go out of the team. In addition, new ownership didn't value the Oriole Way; they didn't understand the importance of growing and tending a team, player by player, as in the old days. The new way of thinking, by now pretty much standard in all the major clubs, was that you could buy a team, position by position.[12]

I went to only one game in 1984. I hadn't made a conscious decision not to go, and of course I still loved my Birds. I didn't abandon them because they were losing. Yet, as quickly and mysteriously as the team had fallen apart, I'd lost interest in baseball. I didn't even enjoy reading the sports pages as much as I used to: the writers had begun to sour on the team.

It seemed the Birds had taken me as far as they could. Just as the Orioles entered another long stretch of bad years, my life was getting better and better. I figured out how to teach, and found that I loved it. I held a demanding administrative job in the university, and began to write my dissertation. Although I wouldn't admit it to myself, I was also taking the first steps away from my marriage. In 1986, I left Baltimore, alone, for the first real teaching job of my career.

After the '83 Series, Eddie Murray had uttered a phrase of Roman simplicity and elegance: "Our strength is just being ourselves."[13] I taped that sentence over my desk. I had succeeded in being myself, a self that no longer filled me with the despair I had felt in 1979.

The Orioles had been my metaphor for overcoming the bizarre and difficult in my life. I had conjured them from words long before I saw them in the flesh. If the metaphor wasn't accurate, if the pictures the sportswriters had painted were more fantasy than fact, did that mean I'd been deluded? I don't think so. I was under the sway of a story. A story that keeps up your courage can pinch-hit for the truth. Story is the favorable wind that lofts a would-be fly ball into the bleachers. Odysseus got into and out of more trouble than any hero; was it a coincidence that he was famous for his stories? Stories are measured not by their accuracy but by their efficacy.

• • •

I haven't lived in Baltimore for more than twenty years, and I've never been even mildly interested in another ball club, in all this time. Yet I've forgotten more about the history of the Roman republic than I have about my Birds. As baseball's Boswell has written, "Football acts can all be repeated. Baseball acts stand forever."[14] Here is one such.

It is October 17, 1983. Eddie Murray, number 33, is coming out of the dugout to do what he has been hoping to do his whole life: win the World Series for his team. He is wearing the club's away game uniform: a homely gray tipped with orange and black. His swooping sideburns are testimony to the barber's art, as is his dark, carefully sculpted hair, hidden now under his batting helmet.

In the dugout, Rich Dauer has just asked him, "Kid, can you guarantee it?" He has said he can, but his wrist hurts. He has told no one how much it hurts, but they all know anyway.[15]

He approaches home plate no more quickly than if he were at batting practice. He adjusts his batting gloves. Finally he steps into the box. Suddenly his languor is gone. He crouches tightly in his signature stance, his center of gravity low. He holds his bat almost at a right angle to the ground, as if he is planning to whack a snake on the head rather than a baseball into the stands.

At this moment, the Orioles' magic years are in their final hours. After tonight, this team will fall apart and not come back together. It will be a very long time before the club has another good season, although the new kid, Cal Ripken, Jr., will stay with the team and play in solitary glory. But what is about to happen will remain untouched.

The pitcher throws a fastball down the middle on a 2-0 count. Murray senses the disrespect. He swings.

Observe the ball now as it rises like a small swift moon, and falls beyond the edge of the Phillies' universe. Eddie releases his bat, jogs around the diamond, and is welcomed home by his teammates.

Elizabeth Bobrick's work has appeared in *Fiction, Salon, The Hartford Courant,* and other publications. She has taught Classical Studies at the University of Virginia, the University of Missouri, and Wesleyan University, where she has also taught nonfiction writing.

• • •

1. Daniel Okrent, *Nine Innings: The Anatomy of a Baseball Game* (New York: Tichnor & Fields, 1985), p. 63.

2. Terry Pluto, *Evening Sun,* June 18, 1979.

3. Ibid.

4. Ibid.

5. Edwin Pope, *Miami Herald,* as guest columnist, *Evening Sun,* June 21, 1979.

6. Kevin Cowherd, *Evening Sun,* October 4, 1983.

7. Terry Pluto, *Evening Sun,* June 22, 1979.

8. Red Smith, *Evening Sun,* October 3, 1979.

9. Tom Callahan, *Washington Star,* October 14, 1979.

10. Terry Pluto, *Evening Sun,* October 18, 1979.

11. Kevin Cowherd, *Evening Sun,* October 17, 1983.

12. *Sun* Reporter Michael Hill presented a succinct analysis of the Orioles' decline and of Baltimore's current lack of interest in its team in "The Golden Age of the Oriole Way," *Baltimore Sun, Perspective*, July 7, 2002.

13. Kevin Cowherd, *Evening Sun,* October 17, 1983.

14. Thomas Boswell, "Why Is Baseball So Much Better than Football?" *Washington Post,* January 18, 1987.

15. On Murray's sore wrist, and Dauer's extracting from him the promise of a win, see John Eisenberg's fascinating *From 33rd Street to Camden Yards: An Oral History of the Baltimore Orioles* (Lincolnwood, Ill.: Contemporary Books, 2001), p. 372.

NOSTALGIA: THE 1950s AND MY MITTS

Christopher Buckley

One of the themes central to all my writing—nonfiction as well as poetry—has always been a cherishing, and so far as I am capable, a preserving of the past as I knew it. As early as I can remember, baseball was a unifying factor in America, a common thread through all levels of society, although of course as a kid in the 1950s I did not think in such grand terms. But even in southern California, where we did not have a major league club, baseball was important (it seemed to me) to everyone—boys and girls, adults and kids, even nuns and priests at the school. In all its black-and-white glory, it was one of the few sports on early TV. We all spoke the language (and what sport has a richer or more varied trove of idiom and jargon?), and to our varying degrees we each, as Casey Stengel said, "participated in the ball field." The main symbol of those times, and that shared and democratic pastime, was of course the baseball mitt. A good glove was a treasure, and anyone picking up one of the classic gloves time-travels immediately back to more modest but glorious days.

G oing *My Way,* one of my favorite films, preserves an America when baseball mattered. That world of the 1940s was carried over, with all its views and values, into the '50s and my childhood—a world for better and worse now long gone. The film opens with kids playing baseball in the street, just a few cars parked or puffing along, and Bing Crosby as Father O'Malley stops to watch "rightfield" for a kid who has to run home. In his autobiography, *Call*

Me Lucky (1953), Bing writes about how he helped Leo McCarey, the writer/ director, develop that character, how he wanted O'Malley to have a common touch, and so O'Malley is a friend of the St. Louis Browns and brings along a baseball uniform and a jacket the Browns (first in shoes, first in booze, last in the American League) gave him. The kids of his parish, whom he has to get in line, love the jacket and the uniform, and Bing takes them to games. People had their doubts about a baseball-crazy crooning priest, and wanted a more pious character, but Bing won the Academy Award for best actor, and the film won best picture. Even the pope approved. Crosby later became a part owner of the Pittsburgh Pirates, perennial losers. By risking venture capital, he hoped he might bring luck to the club, the way—as he points out in his book—he had to the Browns: "I put on the uniform of the lowly St. Louis Browns, and by the time the picture was released, they'd won the [1944] pennant!" One of the first of many photos in his autobiography shows Bing as a teenager in a baseball uniform, his mitt in his left hand gripped tightly to his side.

I remember my first mitt, just a toy really, a pancake of a glove—plastic, brown with some black piping. It wouldn't have caught a radish, but it was my introduction to the equipment that would be indispensable to me and my friends for the next fifteen years, hunks of leather upon which we would hang our dreams and disappointments, the memories of uncomplicated days, like our parents did and their parents before them. And so, like most stories, this is about loss—the end of an era, of a shared feeling, the easy hope of the times, and for me, the glowing emblems of it all, my mitts.

• • •

Growing up in the 1950s, we all played ball—street or school ground, Pony or Little League. The pennant race was a main topic of conversation in any town, any summer, anywhere. We baby boomers rode in on the coattails of our parents' generation, the last kids—almost as if genetically encoded—to play baseball at all times of the year, to take it completely to heart. The ball game was on in the car, on the radio in the kitchen, and when TVs reached the majority of homes we came indoors on weekend afternoons to watch games in black-and-white. I can still remember the packed stands, the crowd coming to its feet as a ball arced over the outfield fence, the white hot dog wrappers blowing along the first-base line in Ebbets Field or out to the pitcher's mound in the Polo Grounds, in that soft gray light of the past.

My father had a small wooden chest in which he kept his few souvenirs. My poet's reaction is to make it a metaphor for his heart—both things were kept locked and rarely opened. Still, sometimes he would open one, which led to the other, and show me his huge Bowie knife, issued to World War II pilots flying over jungles, or the short black cane carved from gazelle bone he bought in Cairo. Sometimes he'd hold up a red ceramic star about the size of a fifty-cent piece that came from the cap of a Russian pilot he'd taught to fly. Fascinating gear for a boy, and I never tired of seeing it.

But the one artifact of his early life I treasured most was his baseball mitt, which he always called his "Professional Fielder's Glove." That tag indicated it was expensive, not something for boys to play with. That glove meant more to him than any souvenir from the war; it held the mental pictures of his youth, the peace and simplicity now gone, when he grew up between the wars, when baseball pumped as naturally, as surely, as oxygen through every boy's blood. The mitt was large, shiny, dark dark brown. I was too young to pay attention to the make, and certainly to the model, status details that would become common parlance in my teen years. "Professional" meant you couldn't buy it in the local department store, and so it was connected to players in the big leagues, a glove they used, that set its owner above others on the field. This was his prize, his trophy of the times when people turned out wearing suits and ties, straw "boater" hats and best dresses to sit in the stands.

I recall that the fingers were laced and that it was not a "split-finger" glove as most were prior to 1950; it was not one of those 1920s gloves, a small black flapjack like Babe Ruth has on his hand in the famous photos. Even in 1955 or '56 no kid had a glove without the fingers laced together at the top.

Recently, looking through vintage baseball glove Web sites and the gloves for auction on eBay, I came across a photo of a glove from the late 1940s or '50s, a brand I'd never heard of, Sullivan Stall & Dean, and I was stopped cold; the computer photo took me back to that first time I tried his glove on and the heel and wrist strap rested halfway down my arm. More than fifty years later, I saw my father's mitt gleaming darkly in front of me.

He never wanted to let me use that glove; he was afraid I would lose it. But as a boy without a mitt and with kids calling to play three-flies-up or hit-the-bat, I managed to wear him down and he finally let me take it out to play.

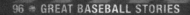

There was a large camphor tree by the mailbox and entry to our drive. I'd leave my gear—cap guns, Indian headdresses, wooden pirate swords— by the base of the tree instead of taking it all the way to the house when we switched from one game to another, one yard or house to the next. My things were always there when I came home—who would want an eightyear-old's toys? So I left my father's Professional Fielder's Glove in my usual spot by the tree and raced up the street to a friend's; it was gone when I came in for dinner. Of course. Exactly as my father had predicted. My first true baseball glove, gone in a day. There were teenagers in the neighborhood to whom—running around with kids my age—I never paid attention. One of them picked up a classic glove that afternoon for nothing more than breaking my father's heart.

It would be two years before I was given another mitt, and it was nothing special: a second baseman's short-fingered model, probably nine inches—maybe eight—from the heel to the tip of the index finger. Even when I was nine years old a portion of my hand extended beyond the wrist strap and brass button. The mitt was branded "Wilson" in black script on the strap but was not endorsed by any major leaguer, and was, after I worked on it, just wide enough to catch a softball, which is all we played then.

Older boys who made the school team had large smooth gloves their fathers bought at Otts on State Street or at All American Sporting Goods on Chapala, the next street over. They carried Wilson and Spalding gloves, Rawlings and Nokona, and some MacGregors, the top makes then and now. There were no discount stores then; cheaper gloves could be had at Montgomery Ward, and Sears sold J. C. Higgins gloves until 1961 when it switched to several Ted Williams–endorsed gloves. But Otts and All American had walls with mitts stacked four or five high, of varying models, twenty or thirty gloves right behind the register where no father with a son along could miss them. The high price of your dreams hung there just beyond reach, beyond any allowance, lawn-mowing, or paper-route money. Sometimes, we'd just walk in and look at the lineup of gloves until a salesman would ask if he could show us anything.

If you were given one of these top-line gloves, it was meant to last for many years; it was almost the 1950s equivalent to what economists now call "durable goods."

By the beginning of seventh grade, my old Wilson mitt had, it seemed to me, grown even smaller. I was going out for centerfield, sometimes playing third, and I'd been haranguing my father for a bigger, regular-sized mitt for at least six months. His answer was always that I had a glove, that we/he couldn't afford it. In hindsight, I see my father going off to work each morning in one of many sport coats from Silverwoods and Tweeds & Weeds, expensive men's shops—Florsheim Imperials on his feet, driving his MG sports car. I see my mother wearing her one cloth coat for years. He had his priorities. But I was stubborn, and obsessed; it was my one topic of conversation as soon as he arrived home from work, and I asked for nothing else. I must have driven him to distraction, for one day late in the fall, I came home to discover the best mitt I (or anyone) would ever own, a new Wilson Bob Feller autograph model, a full-sized fielder's glove twelve inches in length. It was top grain cowhide, a thick but pliant yellow leather with gray piping, made in the USA, the Wilson label on the wrist strap, a black cloth square with gold lettering spelling out the name. I couldn't believe I had won such a battle of the wills and that this glorious glove was mine. That glove fit and flexed like a dream (or choose some other hyperbolic cliché). Why had my father broken down and decided to spend the thirty or forty dollars it must have cost? Later, I discovered, probably from my mother, that he had bought it at Otts and paid only fourteen dollars; he must have walked in on a big sale day, and the price convinced him.

Breaking in a new glove involved myth, ritual, and resources, and sorting through all three. As more modern mitts were made, from the 1940s through the '60s, they truly had to be broken in, as the cowhide and thicker steerhide made a new mitt very stiff. Glove companies developed and sold many different conditioners to soften up new leather and to keep old leather pliable. Lexol was one, and another was Nokona Classic Glove Conditioner, which came in a tube with the company's classic emblem of an American Indian on it. In the late '50s A. G. Spalding offered Speed-EE Baseball Glove or Mitt Dressing Oil in a red can with a plastic spout. From the late 1940s and '50s, Double Play Glove Conditioner contained mink oil and came in a five-inch-tall can. During those years Rawlings promoted Glovolium Baseball Glove Dressing, in a tin about the size cigarette lighter fluid came in, and Sears sold a two-ounce tube of Glove Conditioner—"a special formula for the care of fine baseball gloves." Neat's-foot oil (rendered from the feet and shinbones of cattle) was the one we all knew about, but no one had the money to buy and compare glove conditioning oils. Someone said rubbing bacon grease into the pocket, then baking the glove in the oven at 150- degree heat was the way to go, but I never saw that done. And a kid or two used Vaseline, which some glove repair specialists use even today. Mostly, we broke in our gloves playing a lot of catch, using them, stiff or not, in game after game, and repeatedly throwing a ball into the pocket from about a foot away and gloving it as we sat around talking—almost a nervous habit while watching a game or waiting for one to start.

My amazing new Wilson Bob Feller, however, was so supple I had no problems breaking it in. My only concern was forming a big and sure pocket. The first thing I did was ride my bike down to Jedlicka's Saddlery on De la Vina Street and buy, for a quarter, a rawhide string, one stronger and thicker than the leather the factory used to lace the tips of the fingers together. For my taste, mitts were always laced too loosely, and on any glove I owned I pulled them tightly together. I used a metal pick that looked almost like a dentist's tool, which came from a set we had for cracking walnuts and digging out the meat. I poked through the new rawhide string and then tied it off tight on the little finger. This curved the fingers inward and made a deep pocket from which any ball was unlikely to escape. Then, as many did, I placed a softball inside the glove, tied the fingers around it with string or rawhide, and placed the mitt beneath my mattress for a few days. Thus, the pocket was formed.

The other essential trick to developing a deep pocket was fingering— keeping your index finger out of the index finger slot in the glove. In those years, coaches preached that we should put all five fingers in our mitts and use two hands for every catch, almost as if it were a moral imperative. But you needed to protect your finger and palm from bruising, as that is where a ball most often hit in the pocket. Many kids put their index fingers on the outside of the glove to avoid the sting of the ball slamming into the pocket, but many of us placed two fingers in the little finger slot and moved the other fingers down to leave the index vacant. This gave the glove a more pronounced hinge or closing action, whereas keeping all five fingers in the slots gave you a flat and stiff surface with which to catch the ball. You had to rely on the web to snag a line drive or fly ball, and on early mitts, the webs were small. One way to tell gloves apart by decades is of course by size, and whether the glove is a split-finger or laced, with webbing or not. A 1940s Marathon 4225 endorsed by St. Louis great Whitey Kurowski, a split-finger glove, had only a one-and-three-quarter-inch leather strap between thumb and index finger for a web. By contrast, a Spalding glove I recently acquired, a Jim Palmer/Advisory Staff mitt from the late 1960s, has a web in it six and three-quarters inches tall by five inches wide. After the early 1970s, two changes in mitts occurred. The first is the "fast-back" or "speed-back" style, which eliminated the wrist strap and button or lacing at the end of the strap. It had leather all the way to the wrist with a small thin strap and a cinch to tighten it. On the back of those gloves, just where the index finger meets pocket level, is an oblong hole for the player's finger. As early as 1962, Spalding produced a Rocky Colavito model featuring a small inch-and-a-half loop sewn on the outside of the base of the index finger, also found in Rawlings's "Six-finger" style, which Spalding stole, calling theirs a "TraPocket." Gone were the days of preaching all five fingers in all five slots. By the end of the 1960s, every major leaguer in the world made one-handed catches, and all Little Leaguers were catching fly balls one-handed and keeping their index finger on the outside of the glove. Times change. Glove manufacturing is all about making the biggest and surest pocket possible.

My glove and I were celebrities for a week or so; I had the newest and best mitt at school, and while I did not openly gloat, I must have been beaming the day long.

No doubt I made the same number of stops at third as I did before and caught as many fly balls in centerfield, but other kids seemed to take more notice. I was sure the mitt was magic, and that extra confidence just may have helped with an amazing play or two.

Sic transit gloria mundi—thus passes the glory of the world. I'm not sure which Hall of Famer said that, but it was soon true. We were playing work-ups after school, and I was waiting for the second bus home so I could get my "ups" when the bus arrived and started to load. I ran to the edge of the field to collect my books and sweater when a friend's younger brother, Timmy Armour, asked to borrow my glove. I said I had to leave, but he kept pleading that he was stuck in rightfield and unless he caught a fly ball, he'd never get up. He swore he'd put my glove back in the eighth grade classroom in my desk. All this time, and I hadn't learned a thing about holding on to your mitt. I loaned it to him. And of course it was not in my desk the next morning. I checked the coat hooks in back of the room where some kids hung their gloves—nothing. I caught up with Timmy at lunch and asked him for my glove. He said he'd thrown it in the breezeway by our classroom, where we left our lunch bags before school. I reminded him he'd promised to put it in my desk, but he brushed me off and ran off to play as if my mitt were nothing more than a half-eaten five-cent bag of Fritos. I wanted to wring his neck. Forty-six years later and counting, I still want to wring his neck! No apologies, not the slightest attempt at restitution, as if such could ever be made for that sun-yellow steerhide wonder. To save ten seconds and a few steps, he just tossed it there for any unconscionable kid to steal, and one did. To top it off, the little squirt showed up a week or two later with the same model Wilson mitt. He liked mine so much he'd gotten his father to buy him one from Otts. Numbskull that he was, he came up to me to show me his neat new glove, not to offer it to me for losing mine.

The only solace I took was that, though his was the same model, it was not the same glove. The leather was drier, thinner, and had some creases and wrinkles in it, an inferior piece of cowhide to be sure. Mine had been one in a million.

When it comes to fate and my lost mitts, I often feel as if someone has been stealing my signs, as if I were pitching and getting "pinched" by the ump. I don't know how I told my father, but I must have. That was it. He would never buy me another mitt, and I couldn't blame him. I had signed up for Little League again the summer after eighth grade but had no glove, so I ended up buying an old Rawlings Trap-Eze glove for six dollars from a kid I can't remember. It took all my savings and any allowance I had, but it was a good buy—sun-bleached, cracked, and dry, it still worked—and the kid must have needed the money or had his heart broken by not making his team. The Trap-Eze was originally a midsized infield glove; early 1960s models were endorsed by Charlie Neal of the Dodgers (TG 84) and Vernon Law of the Pirates, and there was even a Stan Musial Trap-Eze model. The glove I bought was standard issue, a larger, later model not endorsed by any major leaguer.

I played a little baseball in high school, mostly games of over-the-line in which you could manage with only three to five players a side by blocking off right- or centerfield. I still used my old Trap-Eze, and when I went off to college probably one of my stepbrothers got it. The 1960s and '70s rushed by with all the bad politics of those times. In graduate school, working several jobs to survive in different places, I didn't have much time for baseball or a game of catch. I didn't care then what became of the glove, but today I sure wish I had kept it as the icon it was.

Time passed and I found myself in Murray, Kentucky, teaching writing at a state university. I made a friend there, Ken Smith, a wonderful fiction writer from Arizona. One day, in the small downtown in Murray at something that would still have to be called a general store, I discovered an aisle with baseball gloves and a few other pieces of sporting equipment. I picked up a Wilson George Brett MVP 390, the A2350 model of select American cowhide with the "Grip-Tite" pocket. It was a midsized glove, eleven inches heel to tip of the index. It was not as big or pliable as my long lost Wilson Bob Feller, but it felt good enough on the hand. There was also a midsized Rawlings mitt, about which I cannot remember much, but they were inexpensive, so I bought both of them along with one baseball so Ken and I could play catch. Somewhere in our early thirties, we weren't giving up on our youth altogether.

I moved back west, I moved back east, and though I had no one to toss a ball with, I kept that Wilson mitt and ball with me, protected and close to new, for a dozen years. Then one day a longtime friend, the poet Gary Young, and I were talking about his oldest son's graduation from Little League to Pony League, and how he was growing out of his old mitt. On my next visit, I brought his son Jake my glove from Murray, and the ball as well, both still in fine condition.

● ● ●

Scratch the surface of nine out of ten men of my generation and they can tell you all about their favorite baseball mitt or mitts from their youth. I checked with my friends from as far back as grammar school and high school. When I mentioned mitts to Francis Orsua, he remembered that his father had bought him a three-fingered Eddie Matthews mitt in 1955, when he was seven years old. Matthews was from our hometown, Santa Barbara, and went to Santa Barbara High School. Francis's father passed away just a few years back and the other day Francis brought out a box of photos. There were, as we used to say, "scads" of photos of Eddie Matthews and Francis's father and uncles and their friends. Long before political correctness, there was Eddie Matthews, who would come home and hang out with his fans, even if all of them were Mexican American, as we said then. They loved baseball and Eddie was a hometown hero, and he gave back to the community.

Francis was not a big baseball player, but he remembered that mitt as if it were yesterday, a glossy dark brown to black infielder's glove from the 1950s, a popular model with a thumb and three fingers instead of four. I recalled two or three of those mitts from grammar school, when we used to share gloves all the time. You placed your middle two fingers in the wide middle finger of the glove. He said he thought it was a Rawlings, but checking on eBay and a few vintage glove Web sites, I found the exact glove he described made by a glove company I'd never heard of, American Eagle, model #7013.

• • •

And so I set about trying to find my Bob Feller Wilson from 1959 or 1960 as well as a Trap-Eze, the unendorsed later model from the early 1960s. What I found was amazing. If you want the best vintage gloves in the best condition and you have $150 to $450 to spend for one, you can check in with Bruce Rogers's Web site, where there are plenty of mitts from the early 1900s. The amazing gloves from the '50s and '60s sell for the highest prices; the famous Rawlings XPG3 Brooks Robinson model, for example, sold quickly at $150. And Wilson's most renowned model, the unendorsed A2000, often sells for double that. On eBay, you can acquire gloves much more cheaply—if you can win an auction; every time I've seen an A2000 or a top Rawlings come up, the bids come fast and furious, and the mitts sell for between $100 and $200. I did manage to place the winning bid for a Trap-Eze Dick Howser TT 85 glove in good condition, but it was not the Trap-Eze model I had in the early '60s, which was a bit larger. This model had the "hinged pad" "Deep Well Pocket" and the "Magic Action Back," as all the models did. "The Finest In The Field!" and "Edge-U-Cated Heel" and "Arch Basket Web"—you have to believe Rawlings had a creative writer on staff, coining the phrases to brand into the heel and pocket, and along the thumb and webs of its gloves.

Despite searching for months through a rotating list on eBay and checking out all the other sites, however, I turned up not one Wilson Bob Feller. The closest mitt I found was a late 1950s model Lefty Gomez Wilson A2044. It was a nice, limber yellow leather but did not have the twelve-inch fingers or deep pocket of the Bob Feller. I've talked to a couple guys who run vintage glove Web sites and they have had lots of Bob Fellers come through, but always the earlier models from old companies like Hutch. My wonderful glove remains a mystery.

I did, however, come up with some great "catch" gloves, mitts in fair-to-good condition at lower prices. One reason for this, I discovered, is that after the 1960s companies started outsourcing their manufacturing to Korea, Japan, and the Philippines. That was the reason the gloves I bought in Murray were comparatively cheap—both were made in Korea. And I did find another Wilson George Brett A2240 glove in great condition, a later fast-back model with the round Wilson label. One way to tell the older Wilsons from the newer is the cloth label; the '50s and '60s gloves have the square label over the wrist strap, and the newer gloves have the circular black label with just a large gold "W" on the thumb. Though this glove was made in Korea, its leather is a more supple yellow leather than the stiffer brown leather of my George Brett glove from Murray, and this is a twelve-inch glove with the newer "Tru-Trap" web and "Snap Action" hinge. Through eBay I also came up with a great Rawlings José Canseco model RBG 36, a twelve-and-a-halfinch fast-back glove in great condition. I figured with his recent book and all the steroid trouble, few people would bid on the Canseco glove, and I was right. When it arrived, I found that it was made in the Philippines. It's a good glove nevertheless, but the gloves that bring the highest prices with collectors—and there are a lot of avid collectors out there—are gloves made in the USA. Usually the cowhide is thicker, but the really thick hides are saved to make gloves for professional players, and you have to know someone to get those. Yet back in the '60s, Rawlings sold a truly professional glove and designated it "Heart of the Hide," and whenever one of those turns up for sale online, it is very expensive. The top price I saw for a glove on an eBay auction was for a Rawlings PRO-1000H fielder's glove, Gold Glove Series, a nonendorsed top of the line model similar to the Wilson A2000. With six hours left in the bidding, there were already twenty-eight bids and the most recent bid was $399. This was a never-used mint condition glove, and collectors were coming out of the proverbial woodwork. On a low bid, I bought a Rawlings KM 6 Dave Concepcion model in poor shape. I figured, should I ever find the time, it would be a good project to restring and restore this shortstop mitt, especially since it is an older model with the single string lacing through the fingers, not the trickier X-lacing. But the wrist strap is about to break through and some of the lacing in back of the "Speed Trap Triple Action" web is broken. Probably this is a project, and a pricey one, for Kenny Jenkins, the professional glove restorer who has a Web site, of course, and who comes recommended by all the sellers and collectors. Jenkins for many years was employed by Rawlings for remodeling and repair, I as-

sume, of gloves used by their major endorsers. These days, he has his own business, and the "before" and "after" photos on his site are impressive and can reel you in if you long for your old glove to look and work as you first remember it. The best eBay buy I managed was also a Rawlings, an XPG16, Chuck Schilling autograph. There were several bidders, and I just went higher trying to acquire a good condition XPG Rawlings, a mitt with first-rate leather. This is a second baseman's glove, as Schilling was a second sacker for Boston. The glove shows wear but is still in fine working condition. I'd love to be able to test it out taking a few grounders at third, but these days I go in fear of bending that low, that quickly, that many times in a row, fearing one time I won't be able to straighten up.

• • •

Collecting is about nostalgia, literally "home-sickness." We'd all like to go back to our youth, for a little while at least. Picking up a few gloves on the cheap, fixing them up, tossing a ball with a friend until the bursitis returns—all of these take you back. If you're from my generation, almost any baseball mitt will have you recalling the days. Put a mitt on your hand, pound your fist in the pocket, and you have your memories—you have your life.

Christopher Buckley is the author of fourteen books of poetry and editor of several anthologies. He has published two books of creative nonfiction, most recently *Sleep Walk* (Eastern Washington University Press, 2006). He teaches in the creative writing program at the University of California, Riverside.

AN ODE TO BASEBALL CAPS

Frank Deford

Each week since 1980 (with a few breaks—I am not the Cal Riken of radio commentators) I've aired a sports commentary on National Public Radio. Unlike most sports journalists, who are communicating with a distinct audience of fans, I know that my NPR listeners form a broad spectrum. Many of them have only a minimal interest in sports. As a consequence, I often try to find subjects that may be idiosyncratic and hardly hard-core sports. My little essay (if I may dignify my remarks so) here on baseball caps is one of my favorites of that genre.

An ode to baseball caps: Oh, baseball cap—

I know. I know. Why in the world am I talking about baseball caps at all, let alone in December, when it isn't baseball season? But, you see, that's exactly the point. Baseball caps are now bigger than baseball. Around the world, they now may well even be the most familiar American artifact, passing Coca-Cola and blue jeans and bad movies. Think about it. How many baseball caps actually end up on the heads of baseball players? Well, I'd wager that fewer people in baseball caps play baseball than people in tennis shoes play tennis or people in polo shirts play polo. Not only that, but baseball caps have risen to preeminence at a time when headgear in general has been in decline: the fedora has gone the way of spats. The beret remains the favorite choice of a few noggins, but as sure as English has replaced

French as the language of diplomacy, so has the baseball cap swamped the beret *sur la tête*—the final indignity to Gallic pride.

Frank Deford

Baseball caps have become so ubiquitous largely because women have taken to them, too. Name another hat that is so unisex. This is largely because of the most brilliant clothing invention since the zipper, namely, the hole in the rear of the baseball cap so that ladies might let their glorious long locks stream through the gap in the cap, absolutely Dr. Seussian. Actually, I'll bet you never thought of this. We shouldn't be surprised that women now wear baseball caps, because as millinery experts have divined, the baseball cap is closest in shape and utility to the old-fashioned Victorian sunbonnet. Visualize that now, right? And it also helps the hegemony of baseball caps that they have the adjuster with the little holes in the back. This way, one size fits all. I have a pinhead. I had an old friend with a noggin the size of a watermelon, so big that we called him the head of the school. The two of us can buy the exact same baseball cap; they fit men's heads, women's heads, big heads, little heads. The baseball cap may be the most universal article of clothing ever designed.

One of the ironic things about baseball caps is that so many people in other sports wear them. Tennis players and golfers wear baseball caps when they're playing tennis and golf. Football quarterbacks put them on as soon as they take off their helmet—so, too, automobile racers. I don't understand, though, why so many people wear baseball caps backwards. This doesn't keep the sun out of your eyes, and the gap in the cap looks foolish on your forehead. Of course, a few young knuckleheads even wear baseball caps sort of sideways. Whatever. What you don't see much of anymore is folks who wear their baseball caps way back up on the head. These are the types who tend to scratch their heads. That seems to have mostly gone out, too. Oh, but it'll probably come back in style.

(originally aired December 14, 2005, on *Morning Edition*)

Frank Deford is the author of fifteen books and two screenplays. He is a senior writer for *Sports Illustrated,* a commentator for National Public Radio, and a correspondent for HBO's *Real Sports with Bryant Gumbel.*

PESÄPALLO: PLAYING AT THE EDGE OF THE WORLD

Caitlin Horrocks

For a long time, I avoided writing about sports. American baseball, especially, has always had so many talented writers to do it justice—people who play the game better, know the game better, love the game better than I ever could. On the field, I'm likely to drop the ball. In the stands, I'm easily distracted by soft pretzels. I don't have a head for statistics, either—I've lost many games of Trivial Pursuit trying to earn that Sports & Leisure wedge. So pesäpallo provided several firsts for me: it was the first species of baseball I encountered that I was actually good at, and the first I felt I could say something about that people hadn't already read. This essay also marks the first time I tried to look at any part of my own life through the lens of sports. Why did my father spend so many hours playing catch with his clumsy daughter? What did it mean to be one of the only Americans in a small Finnish town? And am I ashamed of taking joy in being the twenty-something pesäpallo MVP of the fourth grade? No, I am not.

We're leading by one, but with two outs, when I come up to bat. The staff-student baseball game is a yearly tradition at Päämajakoulu, and part of the tradition is that the game isn't played for any set number of innings. Whoever is winning when the bell rings for the next lesson is that year's champion, so the game's normal rhythms are speeded up and slowed down, tense, the leading team moseying through the batting order and the trailing team fielding with a frenzy. Our opponents are a handpicked lineup of sixth graders, mostly the boys who are hitting puberty faster than their peers. Finnish sixth graders are the age of American seventh graders, and a few of the boys are already much taller than I am, which admittedly is not saying much.

I am buried somewhere in the middle of the batting order, but there's only one runner on base, the school handicrafts teacher, when I come up to bat. I don't remember now which student is pitching, but I believe it was Jukkis, the monosyllabic nemesis of my Conversational English classes. Tall and broad and sullen, with spiked, naturally platinum hair, he's barely talked to me all year. This wouldn't be such a problem except that being talked to is nearly my only function here at Pää-majakoulu. Jukkis, I imagine, after nine months of being asked about his favorite animal, his favorite sport, his favorite flavor of ice cream, finds me as infuriating as I find him. We eye each other balefully, the bright yellow ball seeming to glow in his hand.

Because this is a game of pesäpallo, Finnish baseball, Jukkis is standing beside me, across home plate and just out of range of my swing. To pitch he will throw the ball in the air, at least three feet above my head, and I will try to hit it on its way down. If it falls and hits the asphalt of the schoolyard, that's a ball. Two balls and the batter walks. If it falls and hits the base, that's a strike. Three strikes are an out. I have no intention of missing the pitch, but bats and gloves and balls of all kinds have traditionally not paid me much heed. As a clumsy, pudgy kid, a girl who really did throw like a girl, I long ago convinced myself not to care. On this May morning in Mikkeli, Finland, 60 miles west of the Russian border, 140 miles northeast of Helsinki, 325 miles south of the Arctic Circle, eyeing a thirteen-year-old student across the plate, I care desperately. I bend my knees, raise the bat, my stance the same as in the American game, and wait for Jukkis to fling the ball upwards. I concentrate on its speed, its height, and at the same time keep repeating to myself: *Remember to run towards third! Run towards third!*

The pitching style is not the only thing that separates American baseball from the upstart Finnish version: the base running pattern is also radically different, with first base roughly where third should be. Second is over by first, and third is across the outfield, somewhere in leftfield close to the foul line. The distances between each are different: approximately 60 feet from home to first base, then 96, 108, and a long 114 feet from third to home.

The rules for running the bases are different, too. Technically, I don't even have to run after hitting the ball; according to the rules I can hit both my first and second pitches and just stand there, making it possible to advance two runners while remaining at bat. If I hit a fly ball and a fielder catches it, I will be "wounded," not out. (Three outs or eleven woundings end an inning.)

There are other quirks, too: a triple counts as a home run for scoring purposes, but the batter gets to stay on third and try to score again. Stealing is generally not a good idea; anytime a hit is caught, any runner not touching a base is automatically out. If a runner leads off at second and the pitcher throws to third, the runner is out unless he can physically get back to touch second before the pitcher's throw is caught by the third baseman.

Here in the Päämajakoulu schoolyard we are hardly playing a professional game, and most of these rules are irrelevant, which is just as well—it's all I can do to re-

member which way to run. It's also a burden to know that I am playing to uphold faculty honor, my honor, the honor of "grown-ups," the honor of the English language, the honor of Americans. This year, the year of the Iraq invasion, being an American has been complicated. In Conversational English classes my students have mustered their best English, their best understanding of global politics, to ask me *why*: Why is America doing this? Why are *you* doing this? Without consistent access to English-language news, only dimly aware that the war is even happening, I am the wrong person to ask. But I am the only American my students know, and so they assume, surely, I can explain American foreign policy, and surely, I am brilliant at baseball. In their minds, America is a nation of warmongers and ballplayers.

The crowd of students has been booing the teachers proudly and powerfully, rooting for their classmates, but I seem to divide their loyalties. They are used to encouraging me, soothing my embarrassment, watching me climb back on my skis or stumble through a discussion about the school cafeteria porridge with their "real" English teacher, who thinks it's hilarious to test my Finnish in class. They tried to console me when I got so lost during the Official School Skiing Day that the headmaster was dispatched to look for me in the woods. (In my defense, I had been on skis only four times in my life, all of them in the two weeks before the Official School Skiing Day.) They want their team to win the pesäpallo game, but they also want me to do well. Their enthusiasm, their confidence, is palpable: this is baseball, she's American. Finally, *something* she can do.

"Go, Caitlin!" they yell as I wait for the pitch, and I wonder where they've learned the cheer. Video games, perhaps—a lot of their English is from video games. "Game over!" they occasionally shout at each other on the playground. "Finish him!"

This is the home of Nokia, the neighbor of IKEA and Volvo, a social welfare democracy full of tall, trim, well-educated blondes. Finland's educational system has been ranked the best in the world, its standard of living among the highest. Most of my students look like extras from *Children of the Corn*, pale and golden-haired and hauntingly wholesome. They love the place they were born with an innocence, a straightforward pride I envy. I check over their sentence-completion exercises: Finland is_____. *The most beautiful country in the world. The country with the most beautiful nature. The best country on Earth. A place with excellent four seasons.* They are very big on this, the fact that Finland has four seasons; I try to tell them most of the United States does, too, except our winter does not last six months, our summer two.

My students speak of "going to Europe" on vacations. When I tell them that to Americans, at least those Americans who could find Finland on a map, they're already *in* Europe, they shrug. "Sort of," they say. "But not really." This is a country that for hundreds of years was a backwater of the Swedish empire, then a backwater imperial Russian duchy, then a fledgling independent state in the shadow of the Soviet Union. This is a country that has been left to its own devices when it comes to language, cuisine, literature, sports.

Pesäpallo was imported and reinvented by Lauri "Tahko" Pihkala, a Finn studying in the United States who happened to watch a 1907 Red Sox game. He found American-style baseball frankly boring, but upon his return to Finland, he noticed how many traditional sports were losing ground to modern imports. He decided to create a new game, loosely based on a nineteenth-century Finnish game called Kuningaspallo (Kingball) but named after American baseball—and more exciting, faster-moving, and more competitive than either. Pesäpallo was officially introduced in 1922, and the Finnish National Baseball Association (Pesäpalloliito) was formed in 1930. After a name change or two, the sport settled on pesäpallo, a direct translation (base-ball) and transcription of how it sounded to Finnish ears: to the Finnish, the English "b" and "p" sound exactly the same. (Hence my third grade students' hysterical laughter at the phrase "big pig," and their teacher's enthusiastic shouting at an exhibition match at Päämjakoulu's sister school in Britain: "Good bitch! Good bitch!" she praised the English schoolgirls.)

Pesäpallo eventually became known as the *kansallispeli,* the Finnish national sport, and at least during the spring and summer the title is earned. During the winter, ice hockey takes over; losses, particularly to Sweden, could plunge the entire country into a day of mourning. I never saw pesäpallo inspire such heights of despair or triumph, but it is universally taught to schoolchildren, and in the warmer months it is played in many small town and community leagues, as well as in the professional Superpesis league, which prides itself on its separate-but-equal tournaments for male and female players.

Outside the country, it's another matter. Baseball has the United States, Canada, Japan, the Caribbean, and most of the Western hemisphere. Pesäpallo has Finland,

Sweden, Germany, and Australia. There's a team in New Zealand, too, but it doesn't have the money to compete abroad. The Pesäpallo World Cup in 2006, held in Munich, had only four participants. Fortunately for national pride, Finland won the gold. Indeed, there has been a proposal that in the next World Cup, Finland be allowed to field twelve separate teams, one from each of its provinces, to increase participation and create more competition.

As a small country with a pool of potential athletes only five-million deep, Finland has had to make its peace with almost never being good at anything on the world stage. I once asked a Finn if the national soccer team had qualified to play in that year's World Cup. He burst out laughing. And yet Finns are ferociously proud of their Formula One race car drivers, their curling team, their ski jumpers, the long distance runner Paavo Nurmi, who has been dead for decades, and a sixth-place finisher at the 2006 European Championships in women's singles figure skating. In 2002 a sprinter named Markus Pöyhönen won his heat and made it into the finals of the men's 100m at the European track and field championships, the first Finn ever to do so. He finished fifth in a field of seven, and the country went wild. This was more than respectable. This was enough to get him on the Finnish version of *Dancing with the Stars,* and to keep the sixth grade female students at Päämajakoulu swooning over celebrity magazine pictures of him for the next nine months.

Pesäpallo is one of few venues for athletic prowess Finns have to themselves, or nearly so. By having their own brand of baseball, they have ensured both that other countries will have to compete on their terms, and that they will never have to compete on those of the United States. But they don't see pesäpallo as a consolation sport; Finns fiercely defend the superiority of pesäpallo to American baseball. They won't even be diplomatic about it. To them, there is no contest. They claim pesäpallo is more entertaining, more physically and intellectually demanding—basically, smarter, fitter, faster, better—than baseball. "Are you tired of watching boring baseball?" demands an international rule booklet. "Do you prefer faster and more tactical batting sports?"

To some extent these claims are demonstrably true—pesäpallo games are shorter, with two periods of four innings each, and the ball stays in motion much more. Finns are proud that pesäpallo doesn't reward power hitters: a ball that goes over the fence is counted as a foul. The goal of a skilled batter is to hit the ball to certain parts of the outfield—where the fielders aren't, yes, but more than that, there are very specific plays that require highly accurate hitting to move all the runners into position. At the game's highest levels, teams have playbooks and plans closer in complexity to American football than baseball.

To present the American side of this argument, I defer to sportswriter Red Smith, who had the (mis)fortune of watching a pesäpallo match when it was an exhibition sport at the 1952 Helsinki Olympics. Pesäpallo's inventor, Pihkala himself, threw out the opening pitch. Smith titled his article "Monstrous Infant": "They played a ball game here last night, and if there's a stone left upon a tomb in Cooperstown today it's an upset. . . . [The game] was invented by Lauri Pihkala, a professor who wears a hearing aid. . . . Somebody must have described baseball to him when his battery was dead." Smith thought the game lacked elegance, sense, a coherent strategy, or anything to differentiate it from a bunch of far northern yokels running in zigzag patterns across a field. It is hard to tell, though, whether the game offended Smith's sensibilities simply by being so different from its namesake, or he found it unpleasant to watch, or, perhaps most likely, he simply couldn't get over the most outwardly bizarre aspects of the game. I suppose any true devotee of a sport has a point at which his sensibilities are irrevocably offended. Even Finns look askance at the Swedish brännboll, a version of baseball in which, among other oddities, an unlimited number of players can stay on any one base—the entire batting order, for example, can huddle on first.

Smith also had the luxury of having grown up with the American version of baseball, *the* baseball. But what makes the Finnish sport less legitimate than its precursor? Why is pesäpallo seen as a freakish offshoot of its parent sport, while baseball is given the respect of long tradition and sanctified rules? After all, someone had to come up with baseball, or we'd still be playing "stoolball" on village greens. We just don't know who, despite long-cherished myths like the one about Abner Doubleday's field in Cooperstown. Baseball has a long history and idiosyncratic evolution, as opposed to being the invention of a single man in the 1920s, but baseball is not sacrosanct. Much as Americans complain about the snooze factor in a five-day cricket test match, I never met a Finn who thought American baseball was anything other than the slow-moving dinosaur of the sports world, a woefully unevolved predecessor of his own sport. Even Finns who don't particularly like pesäpallo think

it is a sport far superior, in design and execution, to the American version. Surely, if the rest of the world would just sit up and take notice, if pesäpallo boosters had one one-hundredth of one percent of the money and resources of American Major League Baseball, pesäpallo would conquer the world.

Finland doesn't hold out much hope of this happening, but that doesn't stop the Finns from trying to spread the gospel of pesäpallo, or, as it's now known in younger, hipper circles, pesis. There are a few teams playing now in Estonia, Japan, and Switzerland. The next World Cup is in 2009, so the Finnish Society of Auckland might have time to raise the money to send the New Zealand team.

In fact, there is an entire world of baseball offshoots and progenitors, a family of fringe sports played with bats and balls. Pesäpallo is hardly on the farthest fringe; it already has thousands more adherents than British baseball, for example, a sport played in three cities that touts its yearly "international" championship: a match among Cardiff, Wales, and either Liverpool or Newport, England. Pesäpallo has also outlived some of its sister sports: while nineteenth-century Finns were playing kuningaspallo, Russians were playing the closely related lapta, Swedes were playing langboll, and Germans were playing schlag-ball. Lapta, Russian baseball, dates all the way back to the fourteenth century, as evidenced by the discovery of seven-hundred-year-old leather balls and wooden bats; the pitcher placement is the same as in pesäpallo (perhaps this is where Pihkala got the idea), but the batter must begin his swing with the bat held between his legs. The game survives as an activity for schoolchildren and an official "Traditional Russian Sport." Schlag-ball is similarly hanging on, and even stoolball is still played, if only in Sussex, England. Langboll, alas, has gone gently into the great sports beyond.

It's hard for Americans to realize this anywhere except a dirt playing field in Russia, or an English city green, or a concrete Finnish schoolyard, but American is the not the only flavor of baseball; it's just the one with the largest reach and the most money, and the only one most Americans are aware of.

And yet Finns, as proud as they are of their homegrown sport, understand that it has a clear kinship with the American version, that eight-hundred-pound gorilla. Finns see pesäpallo as a starter experience for foreigners, especially Americans. It is what a Finnish person will try to teach you to bridge the cultural gap; if the two of you can't talk about curling, there's baseball. They bring it up when they aren't sure if you're ready for something like *avantouinti,* a single verb that means going-swimming-by-jumping-in-a-frozen-lake-through-a-hole-cut-in-the-ice. Have you gone avantouinti? Would you like to avantouinti? Did you avantouinti and get hypothermia and nearly die? The Finns understand that avantouinti is approximately an 8.4 on a ten-point scale of cultural adventurousness and assimilation. Pesäpallo is a 1.2. Pesäpallo is to avantouinti what karjalanpiiraka is to kalakukko, both of which are specialty Finnish foods. The former is a rice pastry with butter and the latter is a baked bread bowl full of lard and fish heads.

Since I arrived in Finland at the beginning of the school year, I didn't encounter pesäpallo until the start of the new season the following spring. By that time, I had tried kalakukko and karjalanpiiraka and mämmi, a delicacy that looks like a lump of tar and is a traditional food for Lent partly because its laxative effects help purify the body for Easter. I had also slurped koivunmahla, a traditional spring drink harvested by sticking spigots in birch trees and drinking what comes out. I'd tried to learn to ski, and learned both the Finnish word for javelin-throwing (keihäänheitto) and the location of the world's tallest ski jump (Lahti, Central Finland). I'd attended events including a Moose Raffle and a First Aid Championship, been beaten with leafy birch branches in a sauna, and had a Russian border guard joke about shooting me in the head. By pesäpallo season, I was ready for anything.

The previous spring, with an English literature B.A. in hand and no clue what to do with myself, I had applied for exactly two jobs: teaching English in Finland, and being an apprentice pastry chef at a bakery in Michigan. I didn't speak Finnish, didn't have any Finnish family background—I had stumbled onto the job advertisement online. *Why?* everyone asked me, both Americans and Finns. *Why not?* I answered. Eventually I came up with an answer involving my passionate commitment to teaching and cultural exchange, but "Why not?" was more honest. I was unprepared and under-qualified for the job. I'd made it to my second round of interviews at the bakery when, one morning, the assistant headmaster of a Finnish elementary school was on the phone, telling me Mikkeli was a nice town with only one bear. "I think you will not meet him in the forest. It is not sure that he exists. Maybe you will. But probably not. And if you do you will run away!" This was my job interview: apply for a visa, arrive in August, run from the bear.

My job title is "Assistant Teacher of English," which means various things as the year unfolds. I start out visiting other teachers' lessons: math, science, Finnish, handicrafts, physical education. I'm supposed to engage the students in conversation about anything—numbers, animals, yarn, javelins. I am the school's pet English speaker, the pet American. My job is primarily to be unintimidating, and I trip over my own feet and tongue so often I can't imagine this could really be a problem. By winter, I've graduated to holding my own Conversational English lessons with the older students and teaching the younger ones English songs and games. When a fifth grader tugs on my sleeve one day in the middle of a conversation group and tells me the assistant headmaster/fifth grade teacher wants me to join his phys ed class out in the schoolyard, I worry I've been demoted.

I help haul boxes of equipment out of a shed into the yard that is finally, in late April, free of snow. The kids open the boxes and distribute bats, balls, brown leather mitts. I have heard rumors of Finnish baseball but have never seen a game or the equipment. I allow myself a hint of anticipation. This is not tearing through the forest standing on a pair of someone else's waxed sticks. This is baseball. This I can do.

The teacher tells me he wants me to play, play to win, like I'm one of the eleven-year-olds. He puts me on a team and hands me a glove. For once, he seems to be doing this not as some new way to humiliate me, but because he assumes I will be good enough at the game to provide a productive example for his students. The Finnish winter being as long as it is, there are very few baseball-friendly weeks in the school year, and his students have played only a handful of times in the past few years. No one even asks me if I can play baseball. "Since Finnish baseball is so much easier, you will be very good at this game," he says. "Don't all Americans play baseball?"

For once, I'm glad my father made me play baseball. It was his sport, the one he followed, the one he would have loved to be really good at, the one he would have loved for one of his kids to be good at. My father has two daughters, no sons, and to his credit, the only time I have detected any regret in him over this is when it came to baseball. He had been a rising Little League pitcher, poised to be a large fish in his small hometown pond when his arm was badly broken in a schoolyard fight. He still can't pull his right arm all the way back, but he could spend weekends pitching softballs to his kids, and he still speaks with embarrassing pride about my single moment of sports glory, which happened when I was nine. I don't remember it, but according to him, I pulled off a double play during a game with my summer softball team. I think it was apparent very early on I had no innate athletic skill, but my father didn't lose heart. Our baseball playing, our occasional tickets to Detroit Tigers games, were reflexive but sincere: this was what fathers did with sons, or daughters; this was what Americans did with each other. Faced with a child who read a lot more books about unicorns than she caught fly balls, my father still thought I should at least be able to play catch, to hit an easy pitch.

In American baseball, that's about all I can do. But as it turns out, I can beat the pants off a bunch of Finnish kids. Finnish baseball gloves are larger and rounder than the American version; so is home plate. The pitching stylemakes it much easier to hit the ball. A reporter from the *Chicago Tribune*once asked avid pesäpallo player and Olympic curler Teemu Salo if hethought he could hit a U.S. major league pitch. "I think never," he said. In fact, everything about the Finnish version of the game seems easier. It's like we're playing on the moon, or in some parallel universe. Not only are we all running backwards, swinging at pop-ups, constantly moving, but I'm *good.*It also doesn't hurt that the opposing team is made up of eleven-year-olds. After my first at bat the kids back way into the outfield every time I'm up. I'm still not a power hitter, so the balls don't foul out by overshooting the edge of the field. I can bring runners home without ever going to first base. The only thing I have to concentrate on is remembering to run towards third, instead of the ingrained instinct to run right. My only slipup is missing an easy grounder in the outfield. "Fuck!" I instinctively shout as the ball rolls past me. I look up at my fifth grade teammates, who grin at me. "Don't tell your teacher," I say. Then the bell rings and I go back inside to talk about fourth grade girls' favorite animals: dolphins, always dolphins.

I never did see a live professional pesäpallo game—only televised ones, flipping through the state-owned channels on weekends. The players compete in small dirt stadiums, more like a high school facility than even a minor league ballpark in the U.S. They wear light helmets something like bicycle helmets, and full-body uniforms covered in advertisements, like the ones worn by race car drivers. It's been harder to find sponsors, though, since a gambling scandal a few years back. Some Super-pesis players, frustrated by and struggling on professional players' meager salaries, started betting on and then purposely throwing their games. Like the U.S. MLB strike, the scandal disillusioned fans and drove down attendance.

Although professional pesäpallo is suffering, the amateur version is alive and well. Attendance at the Päämajakoulu staff-student game is universal. A crackling announcement goes out over the PA that I don't fully understand, but I know enough to follow the exodus down the hallway and out into the yard where the children overflow, climbing the wrought-iron fence to stand on the sidewalk outside; they aren't making a break for it, just trying to claim a better view. Another teacher spots me and summons me over to the bike racks, where the rest of the staff has congregated. They have heard I am very good at pesäpallo.

"Yeah, against eleven-year-olds," I say.

My coworkers look disapprovingly at my sandals. Today, everyone except me has brought sneakers. Apparently, my grasp of the Finnish language has not improved

as drastically as I might like to think. I shrug and tell them it's all right; I'll run and field as best I can. The game has been delayed by a choir performance for the retiring woodshop teacher, so it's already unlikely I'll see much playing time. Like baseball, pesäpallo usesnine men in the field; there are lots more than nine teachers, so we send out our best. I insist I am not among them, and to my relief, they believe me. A sixth grade teacher who also happens to be a star player on a regional soccer team makes the first out in the first inning, but the sixth graders manage several runners on base, and one run. The students are making a good showing, and the crowd is ecstatic.

My nonrenewable contract at Päämajakoulu is up at the end of the school year, and I'm not legally eligible to look for work elsewhere. I'd begun applying for teaching jobs in other countries when there was still snow on the ground, when the sun set at two P.M., when I thought I'd vomit if the cafeteria served one more tater tot made of shredded beets. But now, with the beautiful spring weather and hundreds of students laughing and cheering in the sunshine, my heart starts to break a little. Not for the Finnish man I am dating—by spring we both know the relationship won't outlive my job contract—but for this country, for the fifth-place sprinter everyone adores, for lard and fish bowls, for drinking the clear blood of a birch tree, for my generous, self-confident students. *Finland is the most beautiful country in the world. Finland is the best place on earth.* I love them and their moon-baseball, their sport played proudly in four lonely countries. I love them for hitting easy pitches and running backwards and not apologizing for it, for saying *this,* this is the best kind, the truest kind of baseball.

The teachers get two more outs, and the sixth graders grab gloves and take the field. We lead with our best: the soccer star, the lanky assistant headmaster, the school caretaker. Both sides have been playing fast and loose with the batting order; the heavyset headmaster is allowed to bow out cheerfully while I get shoved up to the plate, even though I haven't fielded. We've scored two runs but have two outs and a single runner on base. The children are disheartened, but think they'll have enough time in the next inning to turn the tide. They can afford to cheer for me.

I don't want an American to lose the pesäpallo game for the teachers; I don't want an American to screw up at baseball in front of a bunch of Finnish children. I shoulder the bat and connect with the yellow ball. It bounces in the outfield, and I make it to first/third easily, even with my feet slipping in sandals. Two more batters, two more hits: the woodshop teacher, the long-term substitute for a third grade teacher on maternity leave. The next teacher is thrown out at first as I'm running down the left foul line towards home. The inning ends with the teachers still leading 2-1, and with American honor intact. Our fielders go back out and the next inning begins. Two students make it on base, but two more strike out, and before their side can tie the game, the bell rings. The students howl—not only have they lost until next spring, but they have to go inside to class. The teachers have to go back into class, too, but we march into the school victorious.

In the staff lounge I check my phone minutes and try to decide whether I can afford to make an international call to my father, to tell him I upheld our national reputation in an international exhibition match. I try to figure out how to tell him, if I should tell him, if he will be pleased or offended to learn this: after all his efforts, after being born and bred—every one of us, the athletes and the fans and the clumsy and the dispassionate—to believe that baseball is America's national sport, it is only here on this May morning in Mikkeli, Finland, an hour from the Russian border, three hours from Helsinki, five hours south of the Arctic Circle, running left towards third base, that I am finally the grateful citizen of a baseball nation.

Caitlin Horrocks lives in Michigan. Her work has appeared or is forthcoming in *Tin House,* *Epoch, Colorado Review, The Cincinnati Review,* **and elsewhere. She misses Finnish base-ball, but not Finnish winters.**

FREDDY THE FAN

Sean Wilentz

Baseball is nearly incomprehensible without a sense of history. It's hard not to imagine that at the second baseball game ever played, fans and commentators were already looking backward. Here, historian Sean Wilentz applies his research skills to the role of curator—in this case, of an imaginary (for now, at least) Baseball Fans' Hall of Fame. [L. G.]

One-eyed Freddy the Fan seems to attend every game at Yankee Stadium. He's certainly there every time I am. No matter the weather, Freddy wears his team cap and satin team jacket. He carries a freshly executed cardboard sign, with some clever "Freddy Sez" line neatly composed in rounded, handwritten capital letters, commenting on the team's current tribulations or triumphs. And he passes around his signature items, a dented frying pan with a flaking painted shamrock in the middle, and a spoon just the right size and heft for the fans to smack a few loud rings out of the good-luck pan.

You may not know about Freddy the Fan unless you are a Yankee fan yourself. His real name is Fred Schuman. A native of the Bronx, he was born (as near as I can tell: I've chatted with Freddy, but mainly about baseball) in the early 1920s. According to his less-than-lavish personal Web site, www.freddysez.com (it is the twenty-first century, remember), he lost his right eye playing stickball on 178th Street when he was nine. His all-time favorite Yankee is Lou Gehrig. He has a regular route through the Stadium: first three innings in the upper deck ("because the fans are so enthusiastic up there"); middle innings in the loge; then finishing off with the suits downstairs. He used to make his signs at a seniors' center on Gerard Avenue in the Bronx, though I've heard he's recently moved to Manhattan. A lot about Freddy is mysterious. But he's an important man.

• • •

The Yankees' management does not embrace Freddy publicly, or put him on *its* Web site. Unlike John Adams, the famous fan in Cleveland who thunders away on a bass drum out in centerfield, Freddy never shows up on national television during games. The Yankees' radio announcers have not, to my knowledge, once uttered his name. Yet Freddy gets his message across the airwaves as well as the Internet, as the monotone of spoon smacking pan, sometimes adagio, sometimes presto, soars above the crowd's din. It must be a harsh, bizarre sound to uninformed viewers or listeners. The rest of us, Freddy's fellowship, hear the clanks and know Freddy is at the game and making his rounds. In April, the banging is as glorious as the first robin's chirps. For the rest of the season, it is a form of reassurance.

• • •

I recently read in the *Boston Globe* about an intense fan and baseball historian named Peter J. Nash who is trying to get a Baseball Fans' Hall of Fame started in Cooperstown. Why this idea hasn't yet occurred to the official lords of baseball may say a great deal about the lords' priorities. As long as teams have played for money, there have been outstanding fans, whose extreme passion, loyalty, and eccentricity set them apart from the average devotee. They are as much a part of baseball lore as Abbott and Costello's "Who's on First?" routine, or Russ Hodges's call of Bobby Thomson's "shot heard 'round the world," or any number of other things featured at the Hall of Fame. The main difference may be that unlike the players, managers, and owners enshrined in the Hall of Fame, Immortal Fans draw no salary for their fervor and ingenuity. They do what they do purely for love. It's long past time for that love to be requited and honored. Permanently.

• • •

The new Fans' wing might start with a solitary display, on a glass-enclosed pedestal, of one of Hilda Chester's famous brass cowbells. Chester remains, thanks partly to the mystique of the old Brooklyn Dodgers, the most legendary of the great baseball lovers. For thirty years, beginning in the 1920s, she attended nearly every game at Ebbets Field, surviving two heart attacks and decades of annual disappointment until the Dodgers finally won the World Series in 1955. When, two years later, the Dodgers broke all Brooklyn's heart by decamping to Los Angeles, Hilda Chester—with her stringy gray hair, rowdy profanity, cowbell serenades, and unshakable preference for the bleachers (even after Dodgers manager Leo Durocher gave her a lifetime pass to the grandstand)—was nearly as much the face of the team as the cartoonist Willard Mullins's famous gap-toothed Brooklyn bum.

The story (as told in Peter Golenbock's oral history, *Bums*) goes that Durocher, during one of the team's bad stretches, got fed up with an obnoxious, pestering, disgruntled fan and, armed with brass knuckles, punched him out. The fan sued. Hilda, who adored Leo, testified in court for the defense, perjured herself, and saved Durocher's bacon.

"This man called me a cocksucker," she lied, "and Leo came to my defense."

Greater love hath no fan. If the Hall of Fame's archivists could salvage Babe Ruth's locker, surely they can track down one of Hilda's bells.

Just past the Chester display, the Fans' wing's visitors might enter a large room cluttered with showcases and wall displays. A large exhibit would be devoted to the Royal Rooters, originally a band of Roxbury Irishmen that later came to include Brahmin socialites, and that from the late 1890s until the end of World War I cheered on, first, the Boston Nationals and, after 1901, the Red Sox. The display could include the sheet music for the song "Tessie," whose lyrics the Rooters often twisted around to slander opposing teams.

Elsewhere in the room, there might be megaphones from St. Louis and beer cups from Chicago. The floor could be littered with hot dog wrappers and peanut shells (resupplied daily) that crunch underfoot. The True Life Deranged Fan display might have the .22 rifle (or an exact replica of the rifle) with which an obsessed young Cubs supporter, Ruth Ann Steinhagen, shot her idol, first baseman Eddie Waitkus, in his hotel room after the Cubs traded him to the Phillies in 1949. ("I'm sorry that Eddie had to suffer so . . . ," Steinhagen said before being judged legally insane. "I had to relieve the tension I have been under the past two weeks.") Waitkus recovered and hit .284 in 1950, helping the Phillies to win the pennant. He then achieved literary immortality as the model for Roy Hobbs in Bernard Malamud's *The Natural*.

There might be a small library of books written by or about baseball fans. Philip Roth's *The Great American Novel* would be there next to Malamud's classic. If possible, the Hall's librarian (working pro bono) will track down the manuscript of Zane Grey's story "Old Well-Well," for display (again, if possible) with some memento of the real-life "Old Well-Well," a leather-lunged New York Giants fan named Frank Wood. Near the books would be two grandstand seats salvaged from the Polo Grounds. Interested readers may use them. But empty, the seats would form the Unfortunate Fans exhibit—dedicated not to those generations of Red Sox and White Sox and Cubs fans who never saw their teams win the Series, but to the great theologian Reinhold Niebuhr and his daughter, now well known among the literatias the editor and author Elisabeth Sifton. On October 3, 1951, Niebuhr took his girl to see the last game of the three-game, pennant-deciding playoff between the Giants and the Dodgers. They left after the eighth inning, with the Dodgers comfortably ahead, 4 to 1. So they missed by minutes seeing Bobby Thomson's legendary "shot heard 'round the world"—possibly the most dramatic moment in baseball history.

In one corner of the room might be the sawed-off top of the flagpole that a Cleveland rooter climbed after the Indians won the 1948 Series, vowing not to come down until they repeated the win. (They didn't, and he did.) On a wall would hang the drum played by the Dodgers' Sym-phoney Band to mock knocked-out visiting pitchers trudging off to the showers. Beneath it would be a stuffed goat, a stand-in to symbolize the still-living curse William "Billy Goat" Sianis placed on the Chicago Cubs when the management ordered Sianis and his goat (whom he had placed in the box seat adjoining his) ejected from Wrigley Field during the fourth game of the 1945 World Series—the last Series, to this date, played in Wrigley. From the ceiling would hang dozens of bedsheet banners, with pride of place given to the first one ever to proclaim, "Lets Go Mets!" And, of course, there would be room set aside, one day—but no day soon—for Freddy "the Fan" Schuman's signs and spoon and frying pan.

As it happens, Freddy may be headed to the Hall of Fame even if the Fans' Wing never gets built. An unofficial Yankee fan Web site reported a couple of years ago that, after receiving some inquiries, the Hall agreed to feature Freddy's wares among its cases of sliding pads and tattered ancient baseball cards.

If the story is true, millions of Yankee haters will blanch at Freddy the Fan's being singled out to the exclusion of their own teams' boosters. They will have a point; Yankee haters always have a point. But to complain will be a missed opportunity.

Fred Schuman deserves immortality, but so do the dozens of others who came before him and the ones who will come after him. He might prove the lever to upend an injustice that has lasted too long.

Sean Wilentz is the author of several books, including *The Rise of American Democracy: Jefferson to Lincoln,* **which won the Bancroft Prize in 2006. He teaches history at Princeton University.**

THE INHERENT HUMAN TRANSGRESSION THAT IS UMPIRING: A SLOVENE CASE STUDY

Rick Harsch

By natural disposition an anti-authoritarian personality, I can say for sure that my first outburst against an autocrat outside my home was aimed at an umpire on the baseball field. I'm proud to say that in my memory he was in the right and I was simply emulating Leo Durocher. Even at the time I knew in the back of my head I was acting. The number of authority figures I despise has grown over the years, but baseball umpires hold a special place in my spleen. Denkinger is mentioned in my essay, but generally I hold umpires to be a homogeneous group—it's the managers I remember as individuals: their tirades, their refusals to allow umpires to anticipate calls, expand or squeeze strike zones, or simply exist for very long without comeuppance. From Durocher to Earl Weaver to Billy Martin and now Bobby Cox, who is on the verge of setting the most important record in baseball history—for most ejections—these, my allies, stand for my innate individual freedom.

The last thing a self-exiled American wants to do in his foreign home is come off as an ugly American—or so one would think. Although I try to believe this myself (as a writer living in Slovenia), I can't help but think the truth is Americans *are* ugly.

This should not be taken as an apology, more as something to make my self-aggrandizing stories easier to swallow. For instance, I think it was pretty funny when during a baseball game between the team I manage, Me arice ("swordfish"), and Zaj ki ("rabbits"), the umpire (*the* umpire; we only get one per game) told me I had to put out my cigarette and pour out my beer, and I refused to do so on the grounds that Joe Torre—one manager well known here—drinks and smokes during games. Actually, I don't think he does, but I remember Jim Leyland smoked, and probably Lou Piniella, too. Anyway, my tale had the same sort of effect as citing a Supreme Court decision. This unhumble homunculus softened his face, said "oh," in English, "okay," and the game resumed with me drinking and occasionally smoking.

The game resumed, and umpiring resumed, and if you recall that son of a bitch Don Denkinger screwing the Cards out of the Series in 1985 you'll know just what that means. As the game progressed, this Napoleonesque arbiter blew one call after another, until I was obliged by the laws of baseball to interrupt the game for at least fifteen minutes. The funniest moment came when he got so mad at me he said like a little kid, in English, to my coach, "Tell him I won't speak English to him anymore." So I said to my coach, "Then tell him I won't call him a *pizda* in English either." I would take a major league fastball to the rib cage to witness his befuddlement one more time. Oh: *pizda,* a word used commonly by all speakers of Slovene, literally means *cunt.* I pause to reflect: what could be uglier than to use English in Slovenia to outwit a Slovene man nice enough to speak to me in English given that I'm too dense to learn Slovene? The answer to that is pretty simple: That's no man, that's my umpire.

The Slovene umpire is generally so authoritarian, and his authority is so generally accepted, that it came as a surprise to my own players that I made it a point to engage in at least one savage, prolonged argument per game. What surprised *me* was that even opposing managers would try to stop me from, as one of them (who should have been wearing a long skirt and thick pantyhose when he said it) put it, "taking away from the integrity of the game." Tell it to Durocher, *pizda.* (I have since helped change this craven attitude. Just last year a small mob of my teammates chased an umpire to his car after a game, intending to do him bodily harm—the most rabid player was restrained just in the nick of time, and the umpire made his escape. Earlier that year, a player from one of the old guard teams threw a helmet at an umpire, hitting him in the chest protector, a piece of equipment that should be banned.)

In American baseball, one of the arts of managing is knowing when to stage a moment to get thrown out of a game. In Slovenia, the art I nearly perfected as a manager was knowing how to avoid getting thrown out of the game, since the financial penalty that goes along with that was more than my team could afford. But I had to protect the integrity of this great game from the cultural influences of foreigners, even if they were in their own country. What I try to get across is that the baseball field is a country of its own.

This is precisely the point I was making the one time I did, sort of, get thrown out. The umpire, Franko, bless his innumerable imperfections and may he rot in hell, had scolded my pitcher for swearing when he walked a batter. Within a few pitches he swore again, this time because my catcher threw him the ball as he was walking back to the mound and the ball hit him in the ass. I argued that a man who gets hit in the ass by a thrown baseball has every right to curse. I believe what I said was something like "This isn't a fucking church, you fucking moron." And of course Franko told me to watch my language, which was all the more reason to increase the

voltage as I further explained that language is neither here nor there on the ball field. Soon he told me I was out of the game. I told him that he could not throw me out of the game because he hadn't given me a warning. He told me I was out of the game. I said he couldn't throw me out without a warning: "Don't you know anything about *American* baseball, you fucking nun?" And I smoked a cigarette, and then we got three outs and I went out to coach third base, as I do when we're up, and Franko wouldn't allow the game to resume until I got off the field, and I refused, citing constitutional law (improperly, I knew), and the standoff lasted until the manager of the other team, a good enough guy, talked Franko into letting me stay in the game. Only months later, after the fine was paid, did my own players have the guts to admit to me that we had been fined half the norm, since it wasn't clear whether I had been kicked out or not.

Just as the baseball field is not a church, neither is it properly the space to derive insight into the Slovene character, however much one may be tempted. As I said, the baseball field is a country of its own. Here's a good example. We were playing the Yankees of Slovenia in Ljubljana (I'm really not so bad with Slovene and especially Slovene names, but I can't remember this team's real name, because I simply hate them too much and so refer to them only as something like "those assholes"), a game rescheduled to a Sunday night to accommodate some pettiness on their part, meaning we had to drive from the coast ("swordfish," remember), play the game, and then drive back late on that same Sunday night. I love my team, my boys, but baseball in Slovenia was limited to a four-team league for at least twenty years and this was our expansion team's first year and we had no chance against the established teams (though we regularly kick the shit out of the other new team, our natural rival; my first managerial victory was a 41 to 4 rout). The Assholes, in fact, beat us 39 to 1 in my second game as manager, even after an inspirational speech I gave my team, reminding them that though they had got clobbered in their first game, they had the character and natural ability to beat anybody. Turns out pitching matters as much as they say it does. Imagine one team starting Steve Carlton and the other starting José Canseco. So, 39 to 1. Well, this next game would have been on our territory, but we didn't have a field, so we had to go up there again for a thorough beating. After our sacrifice, we found the Assholes were playing only to get the game over with as fast as possible; once they got the normal eight- or nine-run lead (in the first inning) they started striking out on purpose and not advancing runners on passed balls and that sort of thing. After two innings of this bullshit, I called a meeting at home plate with their manager and the umpire and said we wanted a real game. All agreed, but nevertheless they continued in the same fashion. Finally, in the fourth, I ordered my pitcher to walk the bases loaded when he had two men on. The next batter swung at a ball that went to the backstop, no runners advanced, and so I ordered the pitcher to walk in a run. The batter swung at the first two intentional balls and the inning was over. I pulled my team from the field, informed the umpire that the other team had forfeited, that we therefore had won (the other team's pitcher was throwing a no-hitter, incidentally), and that anyone who felt different could kiss my ass.

The ensuing hijinks illustrate my thesis that the baseball field is a country unto itself, complete with a fully developed sociopolitical system. The guy who most vehemently objected to my decision—being too dense to get how we were being humiliated—was on my team. He was simply out to enjoy a ball game—he was playing for the fun of it!—and was outraged that I had stopped the action prematurely. We may call him the communist. A colleague from the school I am sometimes allowed to work at was on the team at the time, so I said, "Rok, what's your opinion?" "I don't care," he said, "you're the manager." But when he found out we could be fined what would amount to about five dollars per team member, he told me he had changed his mind because "if it affects my wallet I think it's wrong." We may call Rok the capitalist. The biggest pain in the ass about the whole thing was that we had to have a democratic meeting after the game to discuss my unilateral, therefore dictatorial, decision. We may call me the dictator. My closest friends on the team, three of the best players as well, went to get drunk in Ljubljana instead of returning to the coast and would have skipped the meeting anyway. We may call them the anarchists (the people the democratic state most needs yet of course can neither heed nor hear). That leaves the rest of the players, who earnestly discussed the matter to no avail (in that the decision regarding the money was out of their hands and no one would dare depose me). We may call them the everymen, citizen dupes.

I rest my pen. The baseball field could be anywhere: Slovenia, Hungary, Oregon.

Ah, but the outcome of the story. Leaving the field for a moment, we see evidence of Slovenia's Manichean descent and decidedly Balkan character. When I was trying to get a permanent residence visa, the interior minister's coastal representative told me it was impossible—he laughed as he was telling me this—because I needed a work permit, which I couldn't get without a permanent residence visa. "So it is impossible, you see," he said, grinning. Within two weeks I had both the permit and the visa. This is a small country, small enough that even the bureaucrats are humane and what can't be done can certainly be rigged. So, too, with baseball; within a few days everyone in Slovenia's baseball world knew what the insane Me arice manager had done, agreed I was insane and what I had done was stupid, and so decided our team must have forfeited the game because one of our players was hurt and we didn't have a substitute. No fine was issued, and our team had nothing to do with the perpetrated fiction. As far as I am concerned, we won that game without getting a hit.

● ● ●

Because my brain has a sort of apperceptual integrity, I am always aware of its tendency to forge ahead despite its uselessness. One way it does this odd noctambulism is by imagining historical figures as umpires. Try it. If you hate umpires on principle, as I do, you'll find that an interesting paradox arises and even someone as loathsome as Nixon—if only his influence had been limited to the ball field—can somehow become a likeable figure (warning: this does not work with Kissinger, who is demonstrably not human).

Take the 2005 playoffs and that dolt who called strike three on the White Sox catcher A. J. Pierzynski yet allowed him to remain safely at first base. How like Nixon the ump was after the game explaining away his screwup. Yet as a Sox fan, how marvelous, how luminous, I find his ineptitude and duplicity. And think of lonely Dick rambling on in an echoing White House—how *human* to be fooled by Pierzynski's strange about-face and dash. And how Nixonesque to cover up what natural human befuddled behavior had shown through. Imagine whoever you like, and in any circumstances—the game can remove you from life for hours. . . . *The umpire at second, Gandhi, has yet to make the call. . . . It looks like the chief umpire, Bush, has declared the Yankees the winners—Ned, have you ever seen that happen in the first inning with the team down by five? . . . It looked like the tag beat DiMaggio's foot, but Garibaldi, known as the fairest of men in blue . . . This is the first time I've actually seen the umpires lynched, much less the both of them. Sacco made the original call and Vanzetti upheld it . . . the word we're getting in the booth is that Thucydides overruled him, despite having left the park in shame after blowing the call at third in the fifth . . .*

Who do you think would make a better umpire, Tito or Churchill? Though we must condemn Churchill for his warmongering, his contempt for poor folk the world over, and his astonishingly thorough betrayal of the Poles, among many other things, he would certainly look great behind home plate with his mask off waiting for Earl Weaver to challenge his authority. As for Tito, he's Bobby Cox and Whitey Herzog rolled up into one—not an umpire. This is a particularly Slovene slant on my inutile cogitations, for the very route my team takes to Ljubljana is almost precisely that which Churchill tried to convince Tito to allow the Allies to take during World War II. We drive from Istria, up through the Kras region, through the Ljubljana gap, and get our asses kicked by a team from the capital—week after week. From his cave, surrounded by overwhelming German might—think Herzog pinch-hitting Clint Hurdle against a lefty in the ninth, down by two, Hurdle hitting the one important triple of his life and the Cards winning—Tito put out word that Winston was not to step foot on any soil that was inevitably to be Yugoslav. The reason? If the Allies landed there, the territory would not become Yugoslav. The storm surrounding Trieste and the end result, the London Memorandum, more than bore this out.

I don't apologize for taking up a reader's time with my historical daydreaming, which is an inevitable mix of my American baseball blood and my life in Slovenia. My team, composed of young men with Italian, Slovene, Austrian, Bosnian, Croatian, Serbian, Hungarian, Macedonian, Albanian, and at least seven more types of blood if you count my own, now plays its home games on a borrowed field in Italy, about a forty-five-minute drive from here. The players' family homes are on land formerly occupied by Romans, Huns, Avars, Venetians, Hungarians, Austrians, French, Austro-Hungarians,

Italians, Germans, and (some would say) Yugoslavians, that is now called Slovenia. Their traditions are deeply rooted, multifarious, often simple, and often complex; and though for most Slovenes baseball isn't included among them, I am proud that I have added something to the repertoire of these young men.

I have mentioned Franko. Franko made the single worst call I have ever seen in my baseball life. Mirjan Mati , or Gigi, our fastest player, hit a liner into the left-center gap and raced around to third for a stand-up triple, the ball on the relay throw bouncing about nine feet down the line toward home plate, passing Gigi *after* he had come to a rest with his hands on his hips. I didn't see or hear Franko's "Out!" call; I was looking at Gigi and saw his bewilderment, which quickly turned into the pacific, wry smile of a man with a mild soul and a finely tuned notion of where events nestle into context. Even I was calm. When Franko saw me simply looking his way he hurried up to say, "I just can't see everything from here," having a Nixonesque moment. A couple innings later, our Billy Martin figure, Zmago Furlani , lined one into left that went over the flysch rock wall but bounced back onto the field after hitting a wooden fence that keeps bullets from a shooting range on the other side from picking us off as we play. I was bemused, even a little warmed, seeing Franko running up the third-base line to get a better look at what he was about to call a ground-rule double. Allowing my team to riot in protest without me, I went out and retrieved the opposition's leftfielder, leading him literally by the arm up to Franko, and when the guy admitted it was over the wall, Franko reversed his call. What a lovable guy our Franko was becoming. In the next half of the inning I was forced to fill in at first base for Zmago, who had twisted an ankle hopping berserk around Franko before the call was changed. We were well ahead of Novo Mesto, our whipping boys, so if principle meant nothing, nothing would have happened; but a rare Novo Mesto run scored because Franko anticipated the call, as I could well see from where I stood, for the throw beat a runner who not only slowed up but didn't have the wit to slide, and was tagged by Gigi with enough space between his foot and home plate for Churchill to march his army of occupation through. You cannot allow an umpire—ever—to get away with anticipating a call. And then better that hesimply lie about it. In fact, if he anticipates the call, I don't *want* to hear him admit it. Well, we were up about 25 to 2, and it was the last Novo Mesto at bat, and I strolled toward Franko, strolled slowly enough I turned a couple of times toward my boys, and thus saw a most beautiful thing: one here, two or three there, soon all of them, even before I reached Franko, were lying down under the sun, on consecrated baseball grass, having along with me unknowingly conspired in creating a new ritual, one that lasts ten to fifteen minutes, and is undertaken once per Me arice baseball game in Slovenia.

Rick Harsch is the author of several novels, one of which is taught at the University of Tasmania in a course on American film and literature. All of his published novels were translated into French by a publishing house that went bankrupt soon after. He lives in Izola, on the Mediterranean coast of Slovenia, is married to a woman named Sasikala, who has no interest in baseball, has a son named Arjun, who throws harder at age three and a half than Greg Maddux, and a daughter named Bhairavi, who at two years old is showing signs of developing argumentative skills that could lead to a managerial post someday.

FIRST BASE OF LAST RESORT

Matt Wood

I started writing this essay to champion first base as a defensive position and correct the injustice I saw in its characterization as a dumping ground for aging sluggers and weak fielders. As it developed, though, I realized I was really writing about how my relationship with the game had changed. Just as erstwhile superstars shuffle down the Bill James spectrum as their skills decline, I went from thinking I'd play baseball forever to accepting the fact that it was time to walk away. But far from making me bitter or disillusioned, letting go of playing baseball competitively permitted me to be a better fan. Instead of sulking about how I couldn't hit a curveball or had missed a ground ball the previous weekend, I could simply enjoy watching the major leaguers who did it so well. I've learned by now that all relationships change over time; friends move apart, new people come into your life. Baseball has stuck with me, for better or worse.

In the still-sweltering heat of an early July evening, before the sun went down and the hard brown June beetles started pelting the infield dust around my feet, I crouched into my position at first base as the pitcher made his move toward home plate. I had just finished my junior year of high school and was playing for the Owen Dunn American Legion team, Indiana Post #5 in Mt. Vernon. To be picked to play was an honor of sorts; the post had just re-formed the team after a long absence, and the manager was a former college coach who drew players from three high schools in the area.

The righthanded batter hit a ground ball in my direction. It wasn't hit particularly hard, but as it left the bat it had a tight clockwise spin that caused it to slice across the grass toward the baseline. I charged the ball, lowered my glove, and came up empty. The ball trickled through my legs, and the runner reached base safely.

"Nice one, Buckner," I heard from the dugout. I glowered at my teammate Eric, who was sitting near the end of the bench with a smug look on his face. He was referring, of course, to Bill Buckner of the Red Sox, who let a weak grounder by the Mets' Mookie Wilson dribble through his legs in Game Six of the 1986 World Series, allowing the winning run to score and ultimately costing the Sox their first Series win in sixty-eight years. It's still the most infamous play ever made by a first baseman, ruining Buckner's legacy and the defensive expectations of first basemen everywhere. The nickname stuck.

Eric had a knack for getting under my skin. He kept up a constant patter, ribbing me about anything that came to his mind. "Hey, Buckner," he'd say, "is that your sister in the stands? Mind if I ask her out?" or "Why'd you miss that curveball, Buckner, never seen one a them out in the boonies?" I tried my best to ignore him and let my play speak for itself, but a nickname like Buckner doesn't augur happy endings in the baseball world.

First base is a position for aging veterans with bad backs and gimpy knees, the place to hide the worst fielders, the slowest runners, and the weakest arms. It's the place for guys with enough offensive skills to command a place in the batting order but no place on the field. Unlike the other positions, which require specific physical skills—the shortstop must have quick feet and a strong arm; the pitcher, extraordinary arm strength and endurance; the catcher, toughness, brains, and a cannon for an arm—first base is a default position, defined mostly by what its players don't have: namely, the skills required for any other position. A first baseman doesn't even get to touch the ball during the congratulatory toss around the horn after strikeouts; instead he turns his back and smoothes the dirt around the base while the ball goes from third to second, then back to the shortstop, who tosses it to the pitcher.

I started playing first base on my first organized T-ball team in Poseyville, Indiana, in 1982 when I was five years old, and aside from some pitching in Little League and a few emergency fill-in games elsewhere, I've never played anywhere else. I like to think I made the decision because my childhood idol, Don Mattingly from

nearby Evansville, played that position, but I know that can't be the case; at the time, Mattingly was having his first cup of coffee with the Yankees, long before he posted the kind of all-star numbers that made kids like me worship him. The truth is, my dad, the team's coach, decided I should play first base because I'm lefthanded, and because in T-ball, where there are no pitchers and catchers, I would get to touch the ball more than anyone else. And though he would never admit it, I suspect my dad knew I would be the slowest kid on the field, even at that early age. (I probably also helped his decision during one of our first practices, when I fielded a ground ball in the freshly mown grass while playing second base. The other kids and dads were yelling at me to make the throw to first, but I just stood there, brushing the grass off the ball before I threw it.) So, as a lefty who couldn't play another infield position and whose plodding feet made me unsuitable for the outfield, I was left with only one option. Like generations of first basemen before me, my position was determined by process of elimination.

Many players change positions throughout their careers, often early in their professional careers when the trained eyes of scouts and minor league coaches spot traits that make them better suited for a new role on the field. Most moves signal the player's versatility and raw athletic skill. Babe Ruth could have been a Hall of Fame pitcher had he not switched to the outfield so his powerful bat could be in the lineup every day. Hank Aaron started his career at second before shifting to the outfield, and more recently, Craig Biggio moved to second base after coming up to the majors as a catcher. Both Aaron and Biggio became good defenders at their new positions, a testament to their utility.

Famed baseball writer Bill James once devised a "defensive spectrum" that rated defensive positions by their level of difficulty. On the far right of this scheme was catcher, which James determined to be the most challenging position. First base was on the opposite end:

1B—LF—RF—3B—CF—2B—SS—C

According to James, players very rarely move from left to right on the spectrum, but can usually move right to left on the scale with relative success, as players like Aaron, Biggio, Robin Yount, Dale Murphy, Cal Ripken, and Alex Rodriguez have. Still, a move to first base, as you might guess from its position in the spectrum, carries a taint of decay, a connotation of demotion or compromise.

Some star players move to first near the end of their careers to minimize wear and tear on their aging bodies. Willie Mays, Ernie Banks, Johnny Bench, and Pete Rose all spent significant time at first in their twilight years. In Bench's case, the move saved him the punishment of playing catcher every day. Mike Piazza made a similar move in 2004, splitting time between first and catcher during an injury-plagued season. Other players land at first after getting pushed out of other positions by superior defensive players. The Cardinals' Albert Pujols played third until the Cardinals acquired Scott Rolen, after which Pujols made his move left along the James spectrum to outfield for two seasons. He settled at first full-time in 2004, and became an excellent defensive first baseman. And in the 2005 off-season, the Dodgers signed Nomar Garciaparra to a one-year contract and announced that he would play first base. Garciaparra was once considered one of the best shortstops in the game while playing for the Red Sox, but struggled defensively after being traded to the Cubs, eventually moving to third base at the end of 2005. Little worry for him as he joined the Dodgers, though. He expected to learn to play first base in just three months.

I was oblivious to the long tradition of putting the slowest, clumsiest players at first base when I began my baseball career. In my mind, it was the best position on the field. I was playing first base! The first one! Everyone had to come through me, and almost every ball hit on the infield eventually had to be thrown to me, too. Why shouldn't I be proud to play there? After all, my favorite player, Mattingly, won nine Gold Gloves playing first, second only to Keith Hernandez, who won eleven, six of them playing for the Cardinals, my favorite team.

I started paying attention to defensive technique in Little League, where I learned the basics of fielding grounders and began mastering the art of The Stretch. This move—stretching your glove hand and foot in the direction of the throw in order to catch it sooner and beat the runner—is simple but comes in a surprising number of variations. You have to judge the speed and direction of the throw to know when and where to stretch. Is the ball coming in wide? Will you be able to keep your foot on the bag and make the catch, or should you concede the base to the runner to prevent the ball from going out of play? The Stretch can often require the footwork of a ballerina. A high throw might cause you to reach into the air and pirouette as you tiptoe the bag, or you might have time to jump and make a stab with your toe as you land. You might even end up doing the splits to reach as far forward as possible to beat a speedy runner.

In Little League, where the infielders don't exactly have major league arms, The Stretch, along with its counterpart, The Scoop, often means the difference between an out and an error. The Scoop—catching an errant throw by "scooping" it out of the dirt—is the first baseman's best-known defensive weapon. The official rules of scoring are kind to the first baseman; most throws he can't catch result in an error on the thrower. Still, if he had to practice just one defensive play, a first baseman would perfect The Scoop, not so much because it prevents base runners but because a missed Scoop makes him look so bad. It is such an integral part of the first base-man's repertoire, like a layup for a basketball center, that he is expected to pull out every throw, no matter how bad.

To make The Scoop properly, you should keep your glove low to the ground, watching the ball all the way in and catching it just after it bounces. The degree of difficulty depends on where the ball is thrown, the worst place being straight at your shins. In fact, first basemen wear a special glove made specifically to help them scoop bad throws. Whereas most gloves have five fingers stitched together to approximate a hand, the first base glove resembles a wide, flattened lobster claw. Instead of four fingers, it has a round paddle opposing the thumb that can act like a shovel, scoop-ing up a handful of infield dirt along with a poorly thrown baseball. After the round, padded catcher's mitt, it's the most distinctive glove on the field. I got my first one when I was thirteen and starting to play in Senior League, a new league for junior high kids. I was excited about the glove and how it affirmed my special position on the field, not at all concerned with the irony that the autograph stamped in the pocket of my lefthanded glove was that of Mark McGwire, a righthanded player who had converted to first from the pitching mound and third base.

Despite my fancy glove, however, I was never particularly good at The Scoop. Too many short hops off the inside of my knee had made me skittish. Ignoring the cardinal rule of the game—Don't Be Afraid of the Ball—I would turn my head and swing my glove upward hoping to catch the ball with a flourish. Unsurprisingly, I often missed, and betrayed my slow feet as I ran into foul territory to chase the er-rant throw.

Runners couldn't lead off the base in Little League, but in Senior League, as would-be Rickey Hendersons took their first few cautious steps off the base, I got to stand behind them and point my glove at the pitcher. There isn't much technique to making pickoff plays, just a catch and a tag, but it is a rare opportunity for one player to legally hit another as hard as he can. I enjoyed pounding the diving runners on the back, answering their complaints by daring them to do the same as I took a three-inch lead the next time I reached base. Holding runners on base was far less fun than I thought it would be, though, because it mostly meant that I was out of position for pitches. On those blistering Indiana summer afternoons, as my perennially bad teams suffered through long at bats by the other team, I tired of running back and forth to the base, and ended up missing some of the most routine grounders.

Demoting liabilities to first base is primarily a National League phenomenon, since American League teams can dump their defensive white elephants into the designated hitter slot. The White Sox took the glove out of Frank Thomas's hands, as the Mariners did with Edgar Martinez and the Brewers, Blue Jays, and Twins all did

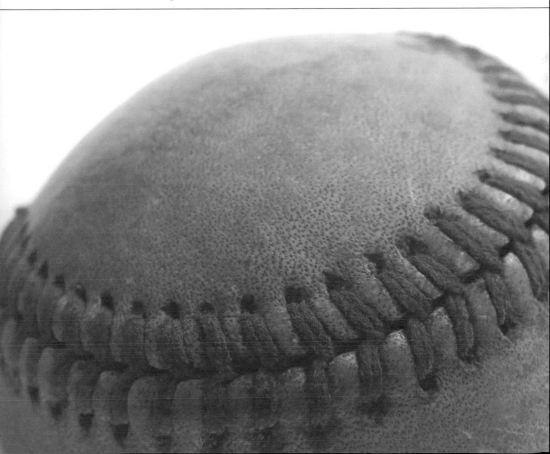

with Paul Molitor. But American League first base purists have to endure the special torment of watching a manager struggle with his lineup in the World Series when the games are played in the National League park, sans DH. In 2004, Terry Francona of the Red Sox opted to bench his team's first baseman and leader, Kevin Millar, so that DH David Ortiz could play there and stay in the lineup for Games 3 and 4 in St. Louis. Ortiz was considered such a bad fielder that some Red Sox fans feared he alone could jeopardize the team's chances of winning the Series. In fact, despite his clutch offensive heroics in the AL Championship Series against the Yankees, Francona pulled Ortiz late in both games for defensive replacement Doug Mientkiewicz. The gamble paid off, as the Red Sox won four straight, squashing my hopes that Ortiz would shed light on the importance of first base defense by making a fatal error, handing a game to my beloved Cardinals and costing Boston the Series, just as a certain outfielder–turned–first baseman did in 1986.

Like any young baseball player, if I could add up all the hours I spent practicing the game, the time I spent perfecting my swing would dwarf what I spent fielding grounders or working on defense. To most kids, including me for a time, hitting was the only fun part of the game, whereas playing defense felt like a necessary evil in between at bats. The longer I played first, though, the more pride I took in my place on the diamond. I loved practicing the arcane footwork around the bag, brandishing my special glove. In high school I started wearing black wristbands—Franklins, just like Mattingly wore—on my forearms just below the elbow, smearing eye black on my cheekbones, and pulling my sweat-stained cap low over my eyes, trying to affect a menacing look to oncoming base runners.

I was lucky enough to make the varsity team as a sophomore in high school, mainly because of my bat and not my glove. I had what the coaches called a "pretty" swing, which I have since learned is a compliment laid on any halfway competent lefthanded hitter. I really was a good hitter, though, perfecting that swing with countless hours of hitting baseballs into a net in my backyard. I was always able to make contact and put the ball into play, not blessed with a lot of power but enough to drive in runs. There was an older first baseman already on the team, so I did my part that year by pinch-hitting and playing late-inning mop-up duty in already-decided games. In practice I perfected The Sweep Tag, an advanced variation of The Stretch in which you come off the bag to catch a ball thrown down the line toward home then sweep your glove at the runner to tag him out as he passes. This play is difficult for two reasons: one, it requires enough agility to catch the ball and twist for the tag without losing your balance, and two, if you're one step off you'll get run over. This happened to me twice, the first just a glancing blow but the second resulting in a violent collision with a player twice my size.

My junior year I was the DH all season. I didn't get much chance to use my Mark McGwire glove that year, either, except for the game in which the coach pulled all the starters and made them run laps for making too many fielding errors. Although I played first every day in practice, after two years of minimal game experience I could feel my defensive skills waning. As a senior I finally played full-time in the field, managing to hold my own around the bag, and in the sectional tournament that year, I made the single greatest defensive play of my career. I was holding a runner on with one out when the batter scorched a line drive toward me. I leapt and snared the ball, landing in nearly a sitting position. The runner had guessed wrongly that the ball was going through and was left stranded between bases. I frog-hopped from the squat and flopped onto first base, doubling up the runner and ending the inning. I remember running back into the dugout, head down, listening to the cheers from our crowd, laughing and blushing as my teammates pounded my back. Later that day I drove home the winning run in the championship game, but the memory of that double play remains just as vivid, a singular moment in which all eyes were on me. That play was something only I, at first base, could have made, and I reveled in it.

I entered my second and final season for Owen Dunn that summer on this high note, hoping to continue at least some part of my high school team's success. The prior summer had been a lesson in humility, our team posting a 5-29 record, losing a majority of those games by the "whitewash rule," in which the game is called when one team is winning by ten runs after seven innings. The summer after my senior year, I drove hundreds of miles in my red Camaro to play in desolate, decaying old farm towns like Fairfield, Illinois, and Petersburg, Indiana, fueled by McDonald's Extra Value Meals and gas station candy. We took a beating again, going 6-31 with just as many blowout losses as in the first season.

I managed to put aside my differences with Eric and the other guys from his school that summer, trying to enjoy what I knew would be the end of my competitive baseball career. Like any kid who has ever swung a bat or broken in a new glove,

I had always dreamed I could be the next Don Mattingly, rising to stardom in the major leagues with my sweet swing and Gold Glove. But I was realistic; I knew there was something about the real prospects that I didn't have. I knew it when I played against kids the college and pro scouts in the crowd, with their stopwatches and radar guns, watched instead of me. I knew it when I heard the way a top-notch pitching prospect's fastballs hissed by me when I swung and missed. I knew it when I watched other players hit those towering home runs I never could. I broached the subject of my baseball future with my coach once that season. I was heading to Indiana University in the fall, and I figured he could help me decide if I had a chance at walking on the team. "The first thing they'll do is time you running to first base, so probably no," he said, smiling warmly, sensing I already knew the answer. I nodded, appreciating his candor, and thanked him for confirming my suspicions. He said I could probably catch on with a community college or junior college team, but I didn't want to sacrifice my academic future just to hang on to a pipe dream for a few years longer.

I have one lasting memory from that season, from a game far away from home on a late night in July. We were playing in Switz City, Indiana, just a few miles from where I'd be going to college that fall in Bloomington. Batting in the fifth inning, I swung and connected with that sweet feeling in which you barely feel the ball hit the bat. I watched the ball arc into the night sky toward the gap in right-center. I heard it bounce off the warning track and hit a metal sign on the fence as I rounded first base. I turned to look at the third-base coach as I approached second and he was waving me through. I jogged into third base for a stand-up triple, my only triple since my very first base hit in Little League. We won that game by our own white-wash; I squeezed the final out in my Mark McGwire glove. A few weeks later it was officially retired.

My baseball career had a brief resurgence after college. I moved to Chicago for a job after graduation, and after a year I felt the itch to play baseball again. I had heard about men's recreational leagues in the city, hardball, not softball or the sixteen-inch rubber ball the coed social leagues used. I found the Midwest Suburban League on the Internet, sent an e-mail, and soon I was a Chicago Pirate. We played on weekends all over the city and suburbs, mostly former above-average high schoolers looking to recapture that spark, to relive the way we felt when we first smelled a brand-new glove. I even bought a new McGwire glove, but things didn't turn out quite like I'd hoped. The league was disorganized; umpires showed up late, the fields were poorly kept, and we had problems scheduling games. The Pirates also weren't such a merry bunch. For every player who was happy just to be lacing up the spikes again, there was an ultracompetitive die-hard who didn't get the message that we were playing in the Midwest Suburban League, not the National or the American. Worse yet, after five years away from the game my skills had atrophied. I missed pitches that I used to drive into the gaps. I swung over curveballs and couldn't catch up with fastballs. I made more errors in the field than normal, and early in the second season I injured my left shoulder, and after that I couldn't throw without causing a grinding pain in the socket.

A season and a half of dodging helmets thrown by those overbearing teammates and witnessing my own sad decline on the field sapped my energy to play. We played by a system in which everybody on the team batted and then worked out a platoon rotation among ourselves for playing the field. I usually alternated innings at first base with another player, but as the games wore on during those hot, sticky Saturdays, games in which we were getting drummed just like my American Legion team, I started taking a pass on my turn in the field more and more often. I was tired of getting yelled at by our shortstop for missing The Scoop on throws he bounced ten feet in front of me. I was tired of chasing those same bad throws into foul territory, then jogging the ball back into the infield because I couldn't throw it to second. I had completed my own full shift left on the James spectrum, from potential to futility, without ever changing positions. Some part of me still held onto the idea that if I couldn't play baseball the right way, I didn't want to play at all. One of the friendlier players on my team asked me to help form a new squad the next year, but I turned him down, walking away from the game for good that second season with five games left. I agonized over the decision, fearing I'd regret giving up something that meant so much to me. But to my surprise, the first free weekend after that, I didn't miss it at all.

Matt Wood is a graduate of the Master of Arts in Creative Writing program at Northwestern University, where his final thesis, "Through an Unlocked Door," won the 2006–2007 Distinguished Thesis Award. He lives with his family in Chicago.

YA GOTTA BELIEVE

John Thorn

Looking back on a lifetime of watching baseball, as opposed to a very few years of playing it, I have begun to think that the truly interesting action may be in the nation's armchairs. Why do we watch? What do we imagine ourselves to be watching while our minds wander? Does our seeming torpor belie a Mittyesque version of Dionysian transport? What are the roots of rooting? I skim a flat stone across the pond with this essay, but I expect I will have more to say on this subject in the future.

I have written about baseball for more than three decades now. At first I sat in the stands, looking down at the field and writing about what I saw. Then I began to wonder about what might really be going on, hidden from sight yet discernible from the game's statistical residue. Over time, as the fascination of numbers waned, I gravitated to the game's largely unvisited necropolis of ancient worthies and uncharted exploits, the men who grew up with the game in the years before league play.

And there I settled in, hanging out a shingle as a baseball historian despite the title's queasy echoes of real-estate novelist. I investigated how far back this children's romp with bat and ball really went, how it came to be Our Game, and why so many have registered claims to paternity.

Lately, however, I have begun to think that instead of surveying the fields of play for the Great Story of Baseball I might better have looked at the individuals surrounding me in the stands, and their antecedents, who more than any ingenious lad made baseball the national pastime. It was the spectator—not a Doubleday or a Cartwright, neither a Chadwick nor a Spalding—who transformed baseball from a boys' game into a nation's sport.

Around the time of the Civil War, members of the press used to call the strangely ardent spectators "enthusiasts" or "thirty-third-degree experts concerning the game of ball." (They used to call some of them pickpockets and drunks and rowdies, too.) By the early 1880s the baseball-mad were commonly called "cranks" or "bugs," both terms intended to reference chronic and incurable illness, with more than a dash of lunacy. In the *St. Louis Post-Dispatch* of April 18, 1884, an ex-governor of Maryland noted:

> There is a man in the Government Hospital for the Insane who is perfectly sane on every subject except base ball. He knows more about base ball than any other man in America. The authorities have humored him so that he has been able to cover the walls of his large room with intricate schedules of games played since base ball began its career. He has the record of every important club and the individual record of every important player. . . . He has figured it all out. His sense has gone with it. He is the typical base ball crank.

On the other hand, baseball had also been recognized as an aid to the "moral management of the insane" at the McLean Asylum—then located in Charlestown, Massachusetts, not too far from Fenway Park—and this, one year before Doubleday's purported invention of the game (from *The Friend; a Religious and Literary Journal*, June 23, 1838). When it comes to baseball, evidently, there ain't no sanity clause.

Where the term "fan" came from has long been in dispute, some saying it was short for fanatic—which would be in line with crank and bug—and others seeing it as a truncation of the eighteenth-century term "the fancy," a flock of aristocratic fops who enjoyed slumming with the rabble at boxing matches. I am persuaded, however, by Peter Morris's recently expressed notion that "fan" was a term players worked up to deride their bleacher nemeses, and that it was a trope for the endlessly flapping motion of all those cognitively detached tongues.

"Rooter" was not exactly a term of endearment, either. Today we may imagine that rooting has something to do with attachment to our team and the nourishment taken from its native soil, but in truth the term derives from the bellowing of cattle, the undifferentiated herd to which otherwise rational individuals willingly surrender their good sense at a ball game.

Whatever one calls the baseball devotee—seam head, stat freak, nerd, and geek are but a few of the recent coinages—the object of the epithet, knowing that his detractors simply do not understand, tends to wear the epithet as a badge of honor. For some fans social maladjustment is indeed a lifelong affliction, meriting empathy and respect, yet for an increasing percentage of others it is temporary and elective: a rented costume and mask, a three-hour license to act badly and get sloshed before the seventh-inning shutdown of the taps. To these revelers the game is irrelevant, and the honorable term "fan" does not describe them.

I have written elsewhere about why we root. Suffice it to say here that it is all about vicarious experience, surrogacy, sublimation, and emulation. When we cheer for our favorites or implore them to win we are doing many other things as well: reenacting archaic rites, reliving past glories, transferring powers from our heroes to ourselves, and, by emulating warfare rather than engaging in it, ensuring the future of the world. In sharing an experience that, like faith, cuts through generational divides, boys learn what it is like to be men and men recall what it was like to be boys. The ballpark, even when visited through electronic media, forms a magic circle for all this metaphysical swirl, which underlies not a staged drama or religious rite, with the preordained outcomes of those performances, but a real-life struggle in which risk is everywhere present.

This is what fans do: they congregate (yes, even when alone in front of the television) to invite change, risk, uncertainty into their lives, confronting danger and loss yet emerging to face another day. Spectating is (at a sublimated level, of course) akin to the experience of gambling or mountain climbing—that is, flirting with suicide. In addition to enjoying the vicarious thrill of an uncertain outcome, fans build belief in themselves for the more significant contests ahead in their own lives. Baseball in America is a sort of faith for the faithless, and its seven virtues are the same as those of religion—*faith, hope, charity, fortitude, justice, prudence,* and *moderation.* All these are traits that might sustain a man or a fan.

Adults who come to the game late tend to make rational decisions about which team to embrace, as forty-year-olds might choose a marriage partner; it can be a cold and dispiriting business. A boy, however, selects his team for a range of reasons he only dimly understands at the time, amid a cheerful obliviousness about who is choosing whom. It would not be too much to say that reason does not enter into his choice; it is almost entirely a matter of *faith.* (This applies to girls, too; I talk about boys and men simply for efficacies of style and because I never understood girls or women.) What must be comprehended at the outset, by even the youngest fan, is that a rooting interest is not to be reversed lightly. A youngster who wavers in his allegiance may not amount to much. If his team loses today or tomorrow, or doesn't finish first this year or next, this is a challenge to his faith and endurance, but it must be borne.

A fan's *hope* is the unreasoning, inexplicable love of Krazy Kat for Ignatz: each blow to the head is merely a love tap, binding the victim ever more closely to the assailant. (At least, some call this hope; others will call it neuro-sis.) Maintaining faith, an ongoing, in-the-moment process, can be a struggle in the face of misfortune and injustice ("we wuz robbed!"). But hope is for-ward-looking and, thanks especially to spring training, cyclically renewable. *Charity* enables the fan to appreciate the human frailty of the players. A child may regard these rented champions for our shires as heroes, but a grown-up fan may not. Disbelief may be suspended, especially in April, but a true baseball fan embraces reality before the end of October forces it upon him. Closers blow saves; infielders make errors on routine plays at awful times; cleanup hitters strike out with men on base. Yes, playing the scapegoat is part of the tribal role for which players sign on. Yes, this is the game you played when you were young, and from a distance it still looks easy. But no, you would not have done better in their place. As an attitude borne in silence, charity is commendable; voiced in defense of a player sorely abused in your presence—now, that is a true virtue.

Fortitude is staying until the game is over, even when your team trails by ten and has lost every game for a week straight and the traffic will be murder. In 1973, the same summer the Mets' Tug McGraw declared, "Ya gotta believe," Yogi Berra famously added, "It ain't over till it's over." Less familiar is the knowledge that Berra left early from Game 3 of the 1951 National League playoff and thus missed Bobby Thomson's home run. Fortitude need not be exercised solo; rally caps, crossed fingers, thunder sticks, whatever fetishes you need to get you through the game—they're all okay. Sure, the players are important, but the outcome of the game depends upon *you*. Remember that.

Justice is being fair with others, even talk-radio callers, even fantasy baseball bores, even Yankee fans. Look upon these benighted souls with bemusement. Winning isn't everything, and debilitates character. Let them pursue victory heedless of the ruin that awaits them in the next life. Can they gnash their teeth as you can? Certainly not. Right conduct and proper belief, even in the face of provocation, will get you somewhere (though maybe not with girls). As Mark Twain said, "Always do right; this will gratify some people and astonish the rest."

Exercising *prudence* helps one to avoid excesses of optimism. When Tuffy Rhodes hit three home runs on Opening Day of 1994, he did not go on to hit 486 of them that season. Don't extrapolate from today's good fortune. Don't bet on the law of averages. Think twice about getting that tattoo of today's hero. Don't lead cheers from the stands; the Carnival King dies at revel's end. Be calm and serene even when your insides are jumping with joy because your team has come back from three down in the ninth. This will deter gloating by others when your team is the one that blows that three-run lead in the ninth.

(Okay, just kidding on that last virtue. Ya gotta enjoy. And ya gotta suffer. That's the human condition, not simply the arm's-length world of fandom.) So to toll the seventh of fandom's virtues: employ *moderation* in all things, including moderation. You know that you are not playing shortstop for the Red Sox, though your emotions are racing as if you were. But face facts—there's no stopping that rush of testosterone or fancied pheromones when your team improbably snatches victory at the last. Winning has its rewards; enjoy them, even while knowing, at the back of your mind somewhere, if you can recall where your mind has gone, that losing is the superior instructor.

For this old boy, with more years behind than ahead, baseball is still at life's core. Not in the same dizzying way as when I was ten years old and my beloved Brooklyn Dodgers left town and, more pointedly, me; not in the same way as when the Mets swept to implausible glory in 1969, filling my heart with joy and my mind with the certainty that anything, yes, anything could happen. No longer in the same warming way as seeing my sons become first players and then fans for life. They are grown now, scattered, yet baseball remains a link for all of us. The game is what we talk about when we want to connect not only with each other in the present but also with our past.

Sport replaces faith for some while enhancing it for others. More importantly for Americans, and more specifically when it comes to baseball, sport constitutes family for the lonely among us, and enlarges it for all of us. Barry Bonds and Ted Williams, Pedro Martinez and Tom Seaver, form extended family at dinner tables; ball games of days gone by are stored like holiday snapshots.

Still baseball, after all these years.

John Thorn wrote his first book thirty-three years ago and has since produced dozens more. His next book, *Baseball in the Garden of Eden,* is forthcoming from Simon and Schuster.

TAKE ME BACK TO THE BALL GAME (VARIATIONS ON A THEME)

Warren Goldstein

Looking back over this essay, which I began nearly fifteen years ago, I was again struck by the way the game serves as a repository for adult longing on many levels. As I write now, in mid-season 2007, Barry Bonds is poised to break Hank Aaron's all-time home run record, and beneath the confused, wounded flood of conversations about steroids and race and character, I hear the same deep notes of longing—for purity, nobility, justice, and so much more.

S tar Island is one of the Isles of Shoals, ten miles off the coast of Portsmouth, New Hampshire. On this craggy, windblown forty-two acres (named for its pointed arms) sits one of the last of the great white wooden Victorian hotels that used to anchor the resort towns of the Eastern seaboard; along with its satellite buildings, this is the Star Island Conference Center. We began our August there fifteen years ago, in 1992, at a weeklong family camp where my wife preached and I taught and played in a couple of annual, ritual softball games. It feels like an older America there: saltwater toilets, showers just twice a week; an ancient stone chapel on the hill; talk of pirate caves bubbling around the children's program. The island has an aura of otherworldly magic about it, and we came thoroughly under its spell. The softball played its part, too. We'd been instructed by the friends who hired us to bring gloves, and were eager to play. Leftfield angles up a hill from the hotel toward the water, while rightfield slopes downward toward the main island pier. In a coun-trified improvisation on Yankee Stadium's famous monuments (plaques, really), the island's tiny graveyard is smack in the middle of leftfield, giving rise to complicated ground rules, as well as the occasional odd musings of fielders and spectators.

As players gathered for the first game, I planted myself at third base. I'm not a very good hitter, never having learned how to get any power into my swing. But I did finally, in graduate school, teach myself to hit singles and to play the infield fairly well. I especially like third base, because though I have developed some courage, I don't have much range.

Warming up, I managed to field the first dozen or so grounders that came my way, and felt an inner warmth all too rare in my often frenetic forty-two-year-old life. I'd proved myself to my teammates, who up until then had known me only as someone who talked and taught and wrote about baseball. Since they were mostly men who had known each other for years, and who played more or less regularly, I wanted their acceptance. One of our number had played professional ball; another was hoping a college baseball scholarship would help him make that leap. That we were playing softball, and not baseball, mattered to no one.

My kids—Isaac, then nine, and the seven-year-old twins Katie and Jacob—weren't sure how to think about a ball game their father was playing, and into which they had not been invited. They kept inching forward from their bench along the third-base line. I moved them back. Some of these guys hit the ball hard, I explained; if someone caught a hooked foul ball in the chin we'd be on our way to the hospital. Only there was no hospital; we were ten miles off shore.

And I realized I liked that physical danger, which connects even a medium-se-rious pickup softball game with the much more dangerous game of baseball. Nor-mally people talk or write about baseball as though it's a gentle, open, sweet green game. George Carlin's well-known routine compares baseball's pastoral nature to the warlike, aggressive football.

But if you sink a little deeper into baseball and its history, or let the imagination play a bit, the danger is not so far away. There's the famous incident, of course, when a Carl Mays fastball killed Ray Chapman in 1920. Roger Angell has described beau-tifully the day-in, day-out use pitchers make of the batter's fear. And in a striking pas-sage in *The Boys of Summer*, Dodger curveballer Clem Labine asks the sportswriter

Roger Kahn to step up to the plate during some pregame warm-ups. When the ball comes towards Kahn's head, the young man is paralyzed with fear. After a few more pitches he is so wrung out, exhausted, and bathed in sweat that he has an epiphany: this is the players' game, not his; never again could he think, even in fantasy, he could play the game he was covering.

Fear and death haunt baseball poetry (see my "Inside Baseball" in the Summer 1992 issue of *The Gettysburg Review*) and even paintings of baseball, many of which are about the spaces between the action, between bases—the interstices, the moments you stop and listen when the darkness at the edge of the field nibbles at the small lighted ballpark or stadium.

This Star Island ball field, too, we learned later that day, had been the site of a brush with mortality, in a story that had become central to the folklore of the group that used the island that week each August. Several years earlier a young boy named Jordan—I think he was five at the time—was playing ball and standing, perhaps catching, behind the batter. The boy at the plate took a large backswing and hit Jordan in the face. He promptly dropped, skull fractured, into a coma. He survived a harrowing evacuation by helicopter through dangerous fog. Many months later, Jordan came out of the woods. Fully recovered, he was Isaac's roommate the week we were there.

To my surprise, I found myself savoring that little bit of fear, the notion that there was peril on the ball field, which grown-ups, mostly men, could brave and best, which children could not. And women? Well, there were a couple of women playing that day, and I didn't worry about them—they clearly played regularly and could handle themselves.

Then someone invited my wife Donna to pitch, and the weather inside my little Eden suddenly turned. Donna had been quite a jock in her younger days, and had even pitched on a state championship softball team in junior high—while I tried out for the debate team. But that was years ago, and now I was worried. The pitcher's mound wasn't far way from home plate, and she might not have the reflexes to get out of the way of a line drive. I wanted her out of the way of the same danger I was enjoying; but that meant either changing the level of the game, which I didn't want to do, or suggesting that she sit out, which would have been publicly humiliating to her. My stomach churned, she played a few innings, and (thank God!) the power hitters all hit fly balls.

My confusion must have showed, for afterwards we fought. She accused me of not wanting her on the field. I denied it, of course, and barely even understood this at the time, but of course she was right. She felt she had earned her way onto the ball field as much as I, a proposition to which I assented, reluctantly, rationally, unhappily. (If she'd only played outfield, I thought to myself, all would have been okay.) I was playing a new kind of game for me, partly in my mind, partly on the field—and she didn't fit there. I'd had just a taste of it, but I wanted more. She argued that I wanted too much, that I needed too much attention.

It's true that I was enjoying the attention. There was a large porch overlooking the field, and people set up their rocking chairs to observe and comment loudly on our game. The entire spectacle was taking me back to years I had never had: playing ball, making good plays in public, with spectators, with just the barest scent of menace in the air, so that if you acquit yourself well you've braved something. Oh, Papa Hemingway! You bet I loved it. I wanted more.

She, on the other hand, had only wanted to play the game, to be a part of the group, and to make sure the children—especially Katie—saw their mother on the ball field instead of the porch. With some embarrassment, I realized that whatever my principles, my fantasy went back to a time before women, before domesticity, to a garden—that is, ball field—populated by men. She refused to compete with something so ridiculous, and backed out of the next game. Great. Like winning a fight with your children, winning a fight with your spouse is predictably, uniquely unsatisfying. She didn't even come out on the porch for the big game the next day, between the staff and the conferees, effectively robbing me of the audience I really, not-so-secretly perhaps, desired the most. And as a result, the game itself never quite rose to the same emotional intensity as the previous day's contest.

When game time arrived, the weather had a New England coastal perfection: a hard, clear, deep blue sky from which the sun warmed the field, but left the shade cool. Donna and I had gotten married on a day just like that, ten years earlier. We players lined up along the foul lines, gazed out to the flag in deep right-center, and from the hotel porch a barbershop quartet, perfectly outfitted in striped shirts and straw hats, sang the "Star Spangled Banner." The breeze picked up, the flag flapped toward rightfield, and we could see heads on the railing of a beautiful old schooner, one of the tall ships from the big Op Sail that had been in New York for the Fourth of July, that had dropped anchor in the small harbor between Star and its neighbor, Appledore Island. I noticed one of my teammates wearing the flannel uniform shirt of the old Boston Braves, a team that hasn't existed for nearly forty years. Deep inside the quartet's version of the national anthem I realized suddenly, with eager wonder, that nothing I could see showed me the twentieth century. For any historian this would be a striking feeling. For someone who has spent as much time as I have immersed in the baseball materials of the 1860s and 1870s, it was transporting. So this is what it was like!

And it was splendid. Along the foul lines players hammed it up a bit; we placed caps over our hearts. Behind us the big old nineteenth-century hotel shone white in the August afternoon. Even game time—three P.M.—recalled when the old Brooklyn Atlantics and New York Mutuals used to play; by then the Fulton markets had closed, and the butchers and other food workers who were the mainstay of some of the early clubs had time to wash, take the ferry over to Hoboken's Elysian Fields, and suit up.

This game seemed to promise so much; the Island and the weather were so exquisite that I wanted even more of it. Maybe we've all spent too many years absorbed by the majors, I felt. There's something important here, in this little ritual game: not a paradise, exactly; there's conflict, and desire, and for all I know, venality and cowardice around the corner. But in this context the game invited me—and maybe others—to look at ourselves and wonder what we're missing in our baseball lives, and whether there could be more. Such a vision of the past and a possible future—all at once.

● ● ●

We hadn't planned the summer as baseball time travel, but we had intended Cooperstown to be our next stop, camping this time, so we headed there next, further backward, circling to the origins of our marriage, to the home and nonhome of American baseball. A beautiful town set on the shores of Lake Otsego, Cooper's Glimmerglass, home of the shrine, the Hall of Fame, so deeply intertwined between American male myths: the frontier and the game of baseball. Men stroll the streets wearing children's costumes; children hold their fathers' hands, not knowing what to make of their fathers' excitement on top of their own. My boys were overcome: all this devoted to baseball? They felt as I had at first: that I'd stumbled into a combination of Mount Olympus and the world's largest candy store.

The town's magic conjured ghosts and romance for Donna and me. Cooperstown is where we first vacationed together, camping until rain pushed us into a cabin; it's where I did my first archival research for my doctoral dissertation; and it's where, after a turbulent year, Donna and I went back for a month—and got engaged one evening sipping gin on the shores of Lake Glimmerglass. Of the pictures of Donna over my desk, my favorite is one in which this mere girl (it seems to me now), tanned and halter-topped, short-shorted, sits laughing, legs and arms crossed, on the stoop of our cabin with the odd French name, Le Bourget. To have found a woman who loved baseball and me, and in Cooperstown—I thought I might just have gotten a whiff of Paradise. I had wanted these parts of my life to come together for so long.

I used to serenade new loves with the last chapter of Angell's *The Summer Game*, the way a friend of mine used to read romantic poetry to his. It didn't always work. One afternoon a few years earlier I had met my then-girlfriend in New York at the movies. It was a balmy day for early March, so I wore my Yankees cap (I was still a fan in those days). Her tone matched the look she gave me: "I hope you're not going to wear that much." And a little emptiness opened in my stomach, the way it does when the object of your attentions says something that reveals, with utter and unshakable clarity, the relationship is over. "Every day during baseball season," I replied slowly and sadly.

But in Cooperstown, for the first time, these disparate pieces of my life—baseball and women and my vocation—had got very close together, though not without some difficult times. Although my new couplehood was glorious, it also forced me into some very grown-up decisions I had no idea how to make. When, for example, was I going to decide to marry this woman who loved me and whom I loved? When, exactly, was I going to finish my dissertation and get a real job?

In baseball, too, we experience these contrary pulls. It draws us into a timeless world in which only the play of the game matters: the alternation of innings, the repeated circling toward home; we can relax in the stands and let the tension build slowly, secure in the knowledge it will be back tomorrow or next week or next year. Mortality there is, to be sure, and even danger, but the kind we understand—the kind that's already incorporated into baseball history and folklore. It has a calming effect. There is, of course, the more disturbing world of crime, of drugs and booze and contracts and owners and endorsements and gambling and . . . but, here, inside, all is well.

Alas, games do end, finally. Darkness comes, the batter grounds to second for the third out in the bottom of the ninth, the sudden home run wins it in the twelfth. Then we exit, reluctantly, from the park, out of the magic circle and into real time where life awaits—and there's nothing easy about that. Remember the excitement as we first caught sight of the field? Going the other direction takes something out of us. Has our brief time inside given us enough nourishment to face the world outside?

Even if you're happy in the game, you need to find a way out of the ballpark; you've got to stop circling back home after a while and move on, or at least expand the circle, as Roger Kahn did after his years with the *Boys of Summer;* as I did out of the childhood ballpark of graduate school. Ambition, growing up, manhood—all these take us out of the park, into degrees, couplehood, jobs, domesticity. In his book *Baseball and Billions,* the economist Andrew Zimbalist tells the story of then-Yankees outfielder Lou Piniella's wife saying one night after a Yankees loss: "I'm forty-three years old and I'm married to a fiveyear-old." As Zimbalist notes, "It sounded like something my wife might have said." Of course. In baseball women see us, nearly always accurately, as boys. Frequently, too, we *are* boys, trying to be men, struggling in some way to prove ourselves through the game. If we can succeed at bringing them into the game, there's an erotic thrill that partakes of the forbidden. Love me through baseball, please, don't condescend to it, don't mother me over it. But love me here.

We should have known that a camping trip freighted with so much memory and desire would tempt the heavens, which promptly sent torrents upon us. After days of flooding, campsite mix-ups, raccoon infestations, running up the credit card, and a brief, powerful, contagious stomach virus, we conceded defeat and prepared to come home early.

But we did have one day of sun, in which baseball gave us another ancient image of itself—and ourselves. I had gone to see the librarian at the Hall of Fame, and he invited me to a game of Massachusetts Baseball that afternoon.

The Massachusetts game, as opposed to the Knickerbocker Club's New York game, was the version of baseball played in New England in the 1850s. Sides changed after one out, batters could be put out by being hit with a thrown ball (called "soaking" or "plugging"), and runners advanced around a U-shaped—not diamond-shaped—arrangement of stakes. The batter began his journey midway between first and home, or fourth stake. The first team to reach one hundred runs won the game. For a while in the 1850s it looked as though both games would coexist, but in the early 1860s, a few Boston clubs took up the New York game (no plugging the runner, three outs to an inning, diamond-shaped field), and others soon followed. By mid-decade Union troops had helped spread the New York game all over the country, and the Massachusetts game pretty much disappeared.

A group of pleasant young men and women from Cooperstown and environs had resuscitated the old game, using authentic reproductions of bats and balls. The ball resembles the one used in T-ball: it's soft, leather, black, and doesn't hurt to catch (the game is played without gloves), though it can sting if a fielder plugs you hard, or in the face.

It feels different from baseball, mostly in the extremely rapid alternation of offense and defense necessitated by a one-out inning—the exact reason commentators thought baseball was so much faster a game than cricket, which alternates offense and defense only after all players have made out. But the golden afternoon, the sky washed clean by days of rain, and the lofty trees at the edge of the field, which bordered on the lake—all combined to produce, for me, an image of the Elysian Fields on the banks of the Hudson River, where organized baseball was really born in this country. The scene looked so familiar at first I didn't even realize what I was seeing. I had spent so many years looking at those trees bordering those fields, imagining the games on the shores of the Hudson. And here it was. The real thing. The early days, the days before championships, before the pros, the days before contracts, before gamblers . . . well, maybe not before gamblers.

On the shores of a beautiful lake that had nothing to do with the birth of baseball. Or did it? What about old Abner Graves claiming that his buddy Abner Doubleday actually laid out a diamond in 1839? No, it didn't make sense. Doubleday wasn't even there in the summer of 1839; he left no evidence of playing baseball then; even Graves had no evidence except his memory of a time more than half a century earlier.

But couldn't it have been like this? Except for the women on the field, that is. At the Elysian Fields women came to watch the men. But this felt right anyway. Then there was the question of the children, who wanted to play. They were on vacation, too, after all. This was puzzling and frustrating for me. No matter how far back we went, the same questions came up. Thomas Wolfe notwithstanding, I was perplexed and wondered why there wasn't a home to go back or come back to—a home beyond/behind the present, beyond conflict, beyond divisions and distinctions. At

Star Island the hotel was named the Oceanic—one of the words Freud uses to describe the early feelings of wholeness that give rise to religious sentiments. Couldn't baseball have just a little of this? Here, on a huge expanse of green lawn on the shores of a lake, I was torn, conflicted, decidedly not oceanic. Was this an adult game, or could anyone play? I was nervous about the situation because I didn't know a soul, and the fellow who'd invited me to play had left early for an awards dinner or some damn thing. I played, but watching my kids' disappointment was painful. Boundaries, finally, weren't that much fun. So I asked, and the regulars let them bat a few times and run around the bases—which satisfied them a little. They still couldn't quite see why they weren't on the field, why adults were allowed to do things they weren't, why the game they played a lot more of this summer than we did should belong to the adults. Which should have made me proud, since they were miles ahead of their father, who would have "understood" if the regulars had said I couldn't play.

I tried to explain, prattling on about levels of the game, about generosity and selfishness, about all kinds of things, and decided to keep playing. Still, the conflict was there, and I wanted to know when and where it wouldn't be. Wasn't there a game, an arena, some ballpark where we could all play together?

Unintentionally we'd begun to re-create the history of American baseball. While the earliest players, in the 1840s, played for the sociability and physical enjoyment of what had been known as a children's game, by the mid-1850s they were being overtaken by players who wanted to win "base ball matches" and club members who wanted to watch the most skillful players. Clubs divided into "first nines" (the varsity), "second nines," and the like, while the least skillful were relegated to "muffin nines" (hence the verb "to muff," or miss, a fly ball)—when they played at all. Many bemoaned this development, and by the time professional play had become common, in the years just following the Civil War, the first version of baseball's lament for the "good old days"—when clubs played for fun—could be heard throughout the land. It was also the last time this grief ever referred to historical actuality; thereafter it drew on the mourner's own (no less powerful) emotional history.

The game split the baseball "fraternity" then, too. Some players and their clubs leapt into "first-class" play and professionalism. Others tried, unsuccessfully, to nur-

ture an amateur ethos; still others resigned themselves to being bypassed by publicity and the lure of gate receipts. But these matters were no simpler then than now. Consider the 1870 Brooklyn Excelsiors. In their glory days a decade earlier they had been one of the finest teams in the United States, and had pioneered the practice of paying a player under the table. On July 4, instead of playing a big money match with a professional team, they sailed up the Hudson to Peekskill, according to a reporter, "to avail themselves of passing the Fourth pleasantly in the country, and on a ball field where the surroundings would remind them of the good old times when games were played for the pleasure and excitement incident to the sport." When the "villagers" took the lead, the Excelsior captain, despite his reveries of days past, exhorted his men "to the necessity of doing earnest work," who thereupon "carried the enemy's works by storm." Even allowing for a little Victorian hyperbole, it's pretty clear that the big city types weren't about to let themselves be bested by a bunch of bumpkins.

One hundred twenty seasons later, my family was tripping over the same dilemmas. What were we supposed to do? I'd had just enough taste of medium-skillful softball to want more. My kids had gotten just enough adult pitching (instead of their own) to want more. My wife had played just enough to want more. I felt their desires as competing with my own. The only one in this situation with any self-control was Donna, who, with some frustration, tried to sort out our conflicting wants. We were having one hell of a time trying to fit these together.

That is, until we all went to see *A League of Their Own,* the perfect baseball experience for that summer of our desires and discontents. It, too, got back to a glorious haven of a past, to the youth of now elderly women. In this one movie we got to see good old days, good guys and bad guys days, women and men days, and days of wonder when Titans walked the earth and women played professional baseball. I had arguments that summer with friends who thought it wasn't really a baseball movie, that it was just a Penny Marshall movie, and not even very good history. They missed the point.

What made it baseball was that the girls on farms were being recruited by a traveling scout-salesman. What made it baseball was how hard the recruits tried to make the team, how much of their lives was consumed by the game, how silly the fashion teachers looked next to young, athletic women from all over the country who shared love and talent for the game.

What made it especially riveting for me, I think, was the way it snuck up on the good old days. For most of us, after all, these were not even days long past—they had simply never been. So the film not only excavated this period; for most of America it virtually created this time when women played the professional game. To sit in a theater enthralled by images I never knew existed, of a baseball so emotionally charged that Katie cried for half an hour afterwards, that, paradoxically—and because of the way the good men overcame their own sexism—seemed to create the very Eden of women and men on the ball field that I couldn't feel at Star Island, was transporting. The game these women played was dangerous, both physically and emotionally. There was feeling and glory and money and flesh on the line when they stood in the batter's box. I still found myself thinking a bit critically about how fast they threw the ball, about some awkward stances. But in the main I was with Katie. I cried through half of the movie, mostly through the sheer joy of seeing this game populated, played, and truly loved, by women.

A peek at the garden is sneaky and seductive. It comes on you stealthily, and before you know it, the images on the screen have got hold of you in places you had buried so deeply they might as well have never been born. Or so you thought. Like a taste of the finest wine, like a moment of sexual bliss, once you have that kind of experience, you start looking to have it again.

So we tried again, once more, on Labor Day, at a picnic for our incumbent U.S. representative, on a buffalo farm on the East End of Long Island, where some farms have held out against development pressure and there's still a bit of the landscape that Nick Carraway waxed so eloquently about at the end of *The Great Gatsby*. A ball game was advertised, and the children couldn't wait to get there. We packed up all the equipment, and I suppose I still harbored hopes of one last good (read: adult) game. I wanted some space in the game for kids, but my grown-up fancies had been tickled just enough to want more where that came from. Was this going backwards or forwards in my life? That summer I'd had both experiences, going back to the nineteenth century, but then forward, too: playing not like the clumsy child I had been, but with some adult reflexes and judgment and eyes— thinking about where to hit the ball, how to get a good peg over to first.

After plowing through mounds of sliced buffalo and roast beef and barbecued duck and corn on the cob and coleslaw, people began wandering back toward the ball field. We seemed to be the only people who had brought gloves (I don't think we went anywhere without our mitts that summer), but kids outnumbered the adults, so it mattered less. We picked teams, and the adults clowned while the kids took the game seriously, fighting over the umpiring and their positions and the score. Alternately gleeful and miserable, the kids wanted so much more from the game—adult rules, adult pitching, adult compassion, child competence and heroism—than it was giving.

That time I was better at sublimating what I wanted from the game, too. A few other guys and Donna and I did our best to make it a better game for the kids—good pitching, decent defense, and it was great fun to see them perk up at being taken more seriously. But I couldn't quite get it out of my mind that if I'd had my druthers, it would have been a different game. Somehow, baseball promises too much. We expect it to carry such burdens of history and feeling and fantasy, of relationships with fathers and mothers and children, that any single expression of the game is unsatisfying. In our search for the perfect game, for the team we can love, the player we can idolize, the daughter we can train, the son we can pitch to, the father we can impress, we want wholeness, the oceanic pleasure of the original ball field. Especially when we want these things so much, we tend not to notice the dangers lurking along that path, at the edges of the field, sometimes even on the diamond.

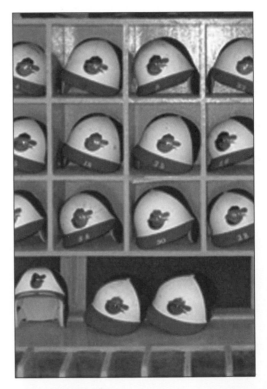

But sometimes the game rewards our search, as in Reggie's third consecutive home run in Game 6 of the 1977 World Series, on a swing that looked lazy yet seemed as predestined as anything I've ever seen in a ballpark. Or when the hulking, ugly female prospect in *A League of Their Own* hits so many baseballs through the gymnasium windows that the scout takes her on in spite of himself; or when your beloved says, "Let's go to a ball game"; or when (as once happened to my son Jacob) a barely four-foot-tall six-year-old has the self-possession to carry out an unassisted triple play without even considering throwing the ball to someone else; or when you look out to centerfield and see a hundred-year-old sloop and a flag in the ocean breeze and the final strains of the "Star Spangled Banner" fade into "Play ball."

Dr. Warren Goldstein is professor of history and chair of the history department at the University of Hartford, where he was the 2006 recipient of the James E. and Frances W. Bent Award for Scholarly Creativity. He is the author of three books: *Playing for Keeps: A History of Early Baseball* (Cornell, 1989); *A Brief History of American Sports* (with Elliott Gorn), (Hill & Wang, 1993); and most recently, *William Sloane Coffin, Jr.: A Holy Impatience* (Yale, 2004), the first biography of the most important voice of American liberal Protestantism in the last half of the twentieth century. His essays and reviews regarding sports, politics, history, culture, foreign policy, and education have appeared in many publications, including the *New York Times*, the *Washington Post*, the *Chicago Tribune*, and the *Philadelphia Inquirer*.

MY GLOVE

Katherine A. Powers

I was born in Minnesota, but spent half of my childhood in Ireland. In both countries, baseball occupied a private chamber of my heart and imagination. It was my private joy, which no one could make me surrender, not by taking me away from the game's native soil, and not by suggesting, as my parents did, that it was not for girls. My first paid-for published work was a roundup review of baseball books, and so I can say without exaggeration that this greatest of games gave me my career as a writer.

My oldest personal possession is my baseball glove, which I bought for eight dollars at Woolworth's in St. Cloud, Minnesota, in 1960, when I was almost thirteen. It was a "modern" glove in that it had shape, unlike the ancient specimens I came across in my grandfather's house that looked as if they'd been fashioned for trolls and exhumed from a bog, or my uncle's first baseman's mitt, a folding horseshoe crab. My glove had—has, I should say—a good deal of rawhide lacing, including four knots tied off on the back of the webbing. Its many seams are beaded, its metal eyelets number twenty-five. It has two leather pulls, one to snug up the thumb, the other to tighten the wrist strap, which is felt-backed for comfort and secured by a metal button that says:

TRADE

H.K

MARK

The strap's black nylon label boasts a "W," which might stand for "Wilson," except it doesn't. The label also says "Made in Japan" and something else I can no longer read. It could be "Professional Model," because that is what is inscribed in the leather of the glove's "little" finger (its largest). The glove's inside surface sports another beguiling "W," as well as "Style 2681" and "[illegible] Set Pocket." I can't remember what sort of "Set Pocket" it was. Deep, I'd say. The inscription has been flattened out of existence by almost fifty years of service.

I bought this wonderful thing secretly, because my father had met the few remarks I'd made about "thinking of getting a glove" with his rote response: "You don't want that." (Other things I "didn't want" were blue jeans, a bicycle, a penknife, a fishing pole, a permanent wave, and a pet of any sort.) A baseball glove? What would I do with it? Who would I play with? Boys at school? I was a girl. Didn't I know that? And *what* was I going to play with? Not a hard ball: we were not having anything to do with hard balls. That's how people got killed and their teeth knocked out and the next thing you knew there'd be a broken window and "I'll be out there doing my act with the putty knife."

For a week or so I fraternized with my new glove on the sly. Behind the closed door of the room I shared with my younger sister—silenced by death threats—I cradled my glove and pushed my face in it, inhaling the deep, fertile leather smell it pumped out along with pheromones, I'm sure. I kneaded it, shaped it, and slammed a ball—a brand-new baseball—in it. Outside the house, around the corner, out of sight, I found a clandestine battery mate, the wall of a brick college dormitory that had no windows on the lowest story. The glove activated all the baseball boilerplate I had amassed from incessant baseball-book reading. Confronting the wall, I flicked off the sign, looked in for another, slapped the glove against my thigh, wound up, and poured one in. Sometimes (if the wall was hitting) I cupped my knee with my glove, waiting for the batter to try to punch one through. I snagged the ball, pounced on it, speared it, whipped it home.

I walked around (out of sight of the house) with the glove tucked under my arm, wishing I could shove it in my back pocket like boys did in books, but of course my pants, when I was allowed to wear pants, had no pockets because my mother had made them, as she made practically all of our clothes. I wished I knew where to get neat's-foot oil, not available at Woolworth's, but no one I could confide in knew anything about that. Another thing I could not do, I might as well confess, was spit in my glove. I could direct the occasional spitting noise at the pocket, yes. But shoot a gob of spit right in there and work it in like you read about? No, I couldn't.

I brought the glove to school, placing it beside me on the old-fashioned bench seat, on top of my books—just like the boys did. In that distant day, or perhaps only in that parochial school, the boys and the girls were not allowed to play sports together at recess, and none of the girls had gloves. But we did play softball and my glove had no problem at all handling the larger sphere. It could handle anything.

Soon enough, unable to keep my love object to myself, I came clean with my parents. Fairly clean, at least: I kept the hard ball under wraps, nestling a tennis ball into the glove's pocket in a prissily responsible manner. I told my father I thought I better tell him I'd gotten a baseball glove. It was a really good one, even though I happened to have bought it at Woolworth's and even though it was made in Japan. I said it was a Wilson and I did not use a hard ball. He looked the glove over, said something unkind about "Made in Japan," and pointed out it wasn't a Wilson. He massaged it with his thumbs, sort of churning them around in the glove, which is what he always did when weighing in on leather quality—one of his specialties. The leather seemed okay, he allowed, but he said he didn't see why the glove had to look the way it did. He whapped his fist in it a few times and then took it with both hands and bent it back and forth as if to reprimand it for the affectation of its deep pocket and slightly curved webbing. He entered briefly into the subject, familiar to all baseball-book readers, of infielders sitting on their gloves to keep them flat so they could turn the ball over fast. I said I knew about that.

He said, "Is this the best you can do for a ball?" I told him that actually I had bought a baseball, but that I only used it against the side of the brick dormitory—you know the wall that doesn't have any windows low down you could accidentally hit. He said that's how you ruin a good ball, scuff it up, leather gets all nicked. I said that was true.

● ● ●

The next big phase of life for my glove came the following year, 1961, with the advent in Minnesota of the Twins. My two brothers, then six and eight, became infected with the baseball bug, though in their own particular way, which, for the most part, did not include playing ball, and certainly not with other boys. This was not really their fault, because our parents did not like the idea of their children associating with other people's children, especially with boys, who might piss against a tree, as had happened once. My mother had said, "That puts the kibosh on playing with boys." Instead my brothers collected baseball cards—not too many, though, because my mother had declared the gum that came with them to be "verboten." One of the boys collected statistics, just collected them and wrote them down. My parents got him a rubber stamp with his name on it followed by the title, "Statistician."

Still, my father, who had been an athlete in high school, felt the urge to toss the old pill around with his sons and teach them the rudiments of the game. Fear of the annihilating ball persisted, however, and, after much deliberation and weighing of consequences, he procured a hardish rubber ball whose destructive power was less terrible than a baseball's, or at least that was the idea. He also got the boys gloves, managing to find suitably archaic versions, possibly from the Goodwill, one of his haunts—though, given the intimate, even germy, nature of a baseball glove, inside and out, maybe they were new. My mother made the boys baseball suits. Being the same sort of person as my father when it came to authentic quality, she made them of genuine woolen flannel, just the thing for Minnesota's ferocious summers of heat and humidity. She made them big so the boys could grow into them and they'd last for years.

So once a week my father, my two brothers, and I got in the Studebaker and drove across the river to the park where hardly anyone went, where there were no baseball diamonds to attract other people's children—and played ball. What ensued beside the brown-flowing Mississippi, among the leafy knolls and upon the undulating greensward, so unsuited to ball playing as most people understand it, is not really mine to describe. I can only say that it had no resemblance to *The Natural* and its scene of prelapsarian baseball. My father called it his "time on the cross"—as he called most family affairs.

I brought my glove to Metropolitan Stadium to see the Twins that year. I sat in the grandstand with my father and his friends, well out of reach of the lethal horse-

hide, wearing the clothes my mother had made for such occasions: pleated skirt and middy blouse. My glove was in my lap, like a handbag.

• • •

The first few years of my glove's long life were filled with bathos. I rarely found satisfactory human beings to play with, and my relationship with the wall ended when one of the dormitory residents complained about the sound the ball made hitting the building. Then we moved to Ireland. My glove came, too. I introduced it to various Irish people who ridiculed it, calling it another instance of American softness in sports—football players wearing armor, baseball players wearing padded gloves. They rolled out the familiar, self-regarding comparisons between American football and rugby, between baseball and hurling (a vicious game played with whirling sticks and a preternaturally hard ball that might have come from my father's nightmares). I looked at my glove and was overwhelmed with homesickness.

Years passed in a generally unfruitful fashion for my glove and me. I moved to London with it, and worked long hours as a barmaid. I had no chance of getting to know anyone who wanted to play ball, at least not when they were sober. My glove rarely made it out of my seabag. I learned later that there had been a regular Sunday pickup game of baseball or softball somewhere in London while I was there. That just made me feel bad: I had missed yet another chance for a different, more baseball-rich life.

Finally, in 1972, my glove and I returned to this country for good, to Massachusetts. This is when we both really came into ourselves and began to live. I finally got some neat's-foot oil. I found people to play ball with. I found, too, for the first time, that it is an unfeeling world out there for the glove owner. I finally had to write my initials on my glove's wrist strap with indelible ink, because some people can't seem to distinguish between their own and other people's gloves. They start trotting off or, worse, driving away with them. When they don't have their own gloves—having lost them through negligence—they use your glove when your team is at bat. They haul away on its leather pulls. They stuff their big hands in the glove and yank the thing off when they're done. Because they have chunky fingers, the inner lining gets pulled out, so now you have to find a little stick or something to poke it back in. It would make you weep, or throw up. I never saw anyone spit in my glove—I can't think anyone would actually do that to another person's glove. But people do leave a lot of sweat behind. Sometimes you don't even feel like putting your glove back on, and you wonder whether real baseball players ever, somehow, wash out the insides of their gloves.

• • •

After a couple of years being back in this country playing ball, a terrible temptation came over me. I can hardly bear to write this down: I thought I might buy a new glove. But when I went to look at the up-to-date models, I was shocked. They looked so big, much bigger than mine, and overweening. They had latticework, hinges, supernumerary integuments and rigging, and all sorts of trademark graffiti stamped all over them, like "Flex-o-matic" and other things too stupid to remember. The fingers of some models extended all the way down the rear of the glove to the wrist, like

the back of a lute or a huge leather seashell. They looked like they played a different game or were pieces of furniture. And they were horribly expensive, soaring into the two-figure range. What did it mean? Were gloves getting bigger to compensate for cars getting smaller?

I shelved the new-glove project for years, until, possessing no daughters, I bought gloves for my sons. By that time, the 1970s and its version of style were only a bad memory, and I found elegant gloves, at reasonable prices, that had at least a modicum of my glove's natural grace.

My glove still has an ancient, raddled grace. Sweat, I suppose, has fused the inner lining to the body of the glove. It could not turn inside out if it wanted to. In fact, it's sort of scraggy in there except in the first finger, which is still smooth from my keeping my finger outside, against the back of the glove, where it has created an abraded hollow. The heel of the glove is ripped where the wrist-strap pull has been yanked too hard, too often, and you can see the padding, looking something like alpaca. When I put my face in my glove I can smell our shared history. The leather's intoxicating odor isn't as urgent as it once was. It is mixed with the cold, mildewy aroma of Ireland and my seabag. There is a biscuity waft of ancient sweat and the muddiness of far-flung playing fields, and, for some reason, an ineffable, but unmistakable, fragrance of books.

Katherine A. Powers was born in Minnesota and lives in Massachusetts. She writes a literary column for the *Boston Sunday Globe.*

SPRING TRAINING LIGHTS

Jake Young

Like many people, when I think "summer," I think "baseball." I'm not sure whether that's the baseball of my youth—playing catch with my neighbor, Patrick, barefoot, losing balls over the bluff, a BoSox matinee on the radio, the play-by-play drifting out to us through the screens of his house's covered porch—or if it's the baseball of today, which offers steroid investigations, fat contracts, year-round updates, expanded leagues, "fantasy" teams, a wild card, and interleague play. This essay attempts to reconcile the two versions of baseball, past and present. I think every fan tries to make the two compatible. And the baseball of old, sepia-toned, usually carries the day.

It's the bottom of the seventh inning, none on, no one out, and the Oakland Athletics' Mark Ellis hits a broken-bat bloop into shallow left-center off Arizona Diamondbacks reliever Jorge Julio. The second baseman takes an angle. The shortstop, Augie Ojeda, number 11, gets a good jump on the ball. He tracks it over his shoulder, running in a straight path under the ball's trajectory in the lights. He is short for a ballplayer, barely 5 8 , but he has good, rapid turnover in his stride as he tracks the bloop; he's got a chance. He gives a hurried signal to ward off the second baseman (who won't make it anyway). It will be a tough catch for Ojeda: being human, susceptible to the drawbacks of bilateral symmetry, he'll have trouble catching a ball that traces his direct path, the ball drawing a bead in line with the fielder's head, the fielder having to cock his head back at a precipitous angle to catch the ball. Baseball players have to make catches like this; so do football players. You watch it: the fielder or receiver runs with his head turned nearly 180 degrees, Adam's apple protruding, hands cradled in front of his chest as if in supplication, as if willing the ball into his mitt or hands, then begins to bend in response to the ball's flight.

There is no wind, the night a still ninety degrees, the Arizona state flag—at half-mast due to the death of Bowie Kuhn, Major League Baseball's commissioner from 1969 to 1984—limp against its pole. If Augie Ojeda doesn't run down the ball, it won't be called an error: Ellis's bloop would fall in for a single and there would be a man on first to lead off the inning. Even so, Ojeda's sprint draws the crowd's attention, a held breath or two. With shallow bloops, there is always a moment when the ball seems to hang in the air, timeless, suspended.

It's March, and the ghost of Willie Mays—who made a famous over-theshoulder basket-catch in the 1954 World Series—has been invoked during spring training. In the Polo Grounds' abyssal centerfield (the clubhouse in centerfield—the distance required of a ball to be counted as a home run— was once measured at 505 feet away from home plate), Mays robbed the Cleveland Indians' Vic Wertz of a 460-foot potential triple (the Polo Grounds allowed for triples; Mays once hit twenty of them in a single season). After "the Catch"—and less well remembered—Mays wheeled and flipped the ball three hundred yards to third base, falling away off his back foot, to prevent the runners on first and second from moving. Mays's play—an overthe-shoulder catch not unlike the one that could take place right here and now at Arizona Municipal Stadium (better known as "Muni")—recalls "The Big Green Bathtub" of the Polo Grounds, the stadium with a full house of history: home to both the Babe and the Mets and the football Giants (1925– 1955) and the Jets (formerly the Titans, 1960–1963), but whose longest and most memorable tenant was the New York (baseball) Giants (1911–1957).

Ojeda's attempt at an over-the-shoulder catch is a convergence of history and memory and something else, something much more literal and earthbound. Of Mays, who recorded the first home run at Muni for the San Francisco Giants, after the team moved in 1957. Of the player, Augie Ojeda, who recalls the time of another Augie (March, the *Adventures* of whom were published in 1951). Of March, that time of year when guys like Ojeda are just trying to make the cut. And then of the ten light poles circumscribing Muni that have presided over not one but two fields, the Polo Grounds from 1940 to 1963, then Phoenix Muni, where they have stood and baked and lit hundreds of night games since. Here they are, transmigrated cross-country to the desert, taking their retirement early, mimicking the migration pattern of thousands of other old-timers on their way west to the desert, where the spare climate might help them eke out a few more years.

The Polo Grounds' light poles were basically evicted from Manhattan, the stadium's demolition scheduled to bring the grandstands (where the light poles were perched) to the ground. On April 11, 1964, the first crews of the Wrecking Corporation of America showed up at the stadium at West 156th–157th Streets and 8th Avenue wielding jackhammers and wearing shiny steel helmets and T-shirts with "Giants" written across the chest and numbers emblazoned on the sleeves (the corporation's manager and vice president, Harry Avirom, a Dodgers fan, wore the number "1"). It would take the sixty-man crew four months to bring the stadium to the ground.

That first day was all smiles and photo ops. Truth be told, the Polo Grounds' demise had dragged on for six years, causing litigation in courts between the city and the Coogan family (the Polo Grounds was nestled in the lee of Coogan's Bluff, which became one of many Polo Grounds sobriquets). The Mets' Polo Grounds finale, September 18, 1963, was the stadium's third, the first being for the Giants when they left in '57, the second for the Mets in '62, before they knew that Shea Stadium's construction had delays and their debut in Queens would be pushed back to '64. That was the attitude as the Polo Grounds came down: let's get this show on the road.

The centerfield bleachers and clubhouses—right about where Mays made "the Catch"—were the first to go, to allow trucks and cranes to enter the ballpark. Crew members who were Dodgers fans joked about how long they'd wanted to bring the Polo Grounds down (Ebbets Field had been demolished in 1960; the same wrecking ball was used on both stadiums). When Dodgers fan Stephen McNair approached the leftfield fence beneath Section 33, over which Bobby Thomson launched the line-drive home run better known as "the shot heard 'round the world" at 4:11 P.M. on October 3rd, 1951, he marked it off and vowed, "I'm going to take that place down myself."

You see, Thomson's three-run homer had knocked the Dodgers out of the World Series and brought the Giants in. (Russ Hodges's call is the most famous in sports history: "Brooklyn leads it, 4-2. Hartung down the line at third, not taking any chances. Lockman without too big of a lead at second, but he'll be running like the wind if Thomson hits one. Branca throws. There's a long drive. It's gonna be, I believe . . ." Hodges then repeats "The Giants win the pennant!" five times.) The game was the third of a best-ofthree playoff, each team taking its home field in the first two. On August 11th of that year (1951), the Giants had been trailing the Dodgers by a seemingly insurmountable thirteen and a half games. Leo Durocher, formerly the Dodgers' manager, led the Giants to a stretch run of thirty-seven wins against only seven losses in the team's final forty-four games, tying the Dodgers for first place and the right to go to the World Series. That the Giants would lose the

World Series to the Yankees was no matter; they'd already achieved the impossible. (What kind of avarice demands more grace when grace has already been achieved? For example, even if the Red Sox had not beaten the St. Louis Cardinals in the 2004 World Series to break the Curse of the Bambino, their comeback from a 3-0 series deficit against the Yankees in the ALCS would have been a legend in itself.) So when that ball took flight at 4:11 P.M. that afternoon, no Giants fan living wanted to see it come down; it meant a heck of a lot to them that it didn't.

With McNair at the ready with his sledgehammer, about to demolish the leftfield fence for the New York City Housing Commission (and Dodgers fans everywhere), the foreman, Abe Gach, called over to McNair.

"No, you don't," he shouted. "Be gentle over there. History was made there."

It wasn't reported whether Gach was a Giants fan or not.

It's the only home night game of the Oakland A's spring training, the lamps of the Polo Grounds' light poles brightening the night. (The A's schedule only one night game during spring training, for the sake of visiting fans who want to soak up sun.) I'm watching the game from a vacant press box with James Vujs (pronounced "voice"), the stadium manager of Phoenix Muni. He's an employee of the city, not the A's. These are his "three outs," which usually occur towards the end of the game when his two-way radio goes quiet and he gets the chance to take in an inning.

For the game's other fifty-one outs, the other eight or eight and a half innings of play, Vujs walks constantly, treads ground from one end of the stadium to the other. His work uniform consists of khakis and a polo shirt. He has a permanent sheen of sweat on his brow, his hair short and combed over. Every March, he goes through two pairs of dress shoes— one a pair of black loafers, the other a pair of brown lace-ups—handling the small hiccups and distractions and slipups and snafus that are a product of nearly nine thousand people occupying the same enclosed space at once.

Hiram Bocachica is batting for the A's now. The lights have illuminated a hovering cloud of smoke slowly drifting over the field from the barbecue behind the leftfield stands, the cloud appearing eerily purple, casting a spooky feeling over the stadium. The home team A's have rallied for two runs in the seventh to close the gap in the score to 8-3, Diamondbacks. Julio delivers a pitch that looks outside from the box. The umpire calls strike three, and the stadium fills with halfhearted booing.

"Spring training strike," Vujs says.

The rally and the inning are over, the game sped along by the bad call. Vujs has taken in his "three outs," and it is time to leave the box and go back to work.

Vujs is in his seventh year at the stadium and, with his team of five men, he makes certain the operation of the stadium during game time runs like inning-work. (His time doesn't run by the clock, it runs by the inning. He doesn't clock out from work; you could say he innings out.) Here, at Muni, his job is minimizing risk—prophylaxis, predamage damage control.

Because this is the only night game of spring training, Vujs has had to deal with more snafus than usual. Twenty minutes before the first pitch, mistimed sprinklers went off in front of the Rock House, nearly dousing people by the Speed Pitch attraction on the concourse. Then, while Vujs was checking out a vomit spill near the gate, his boss, Rob Harmon, who manages both Muni and Maryvale, the stadium across Phoenix and the spring training home of the Brewers, phoned him on his cell.

"James. Do you keep a pregame checklist of things that need to get done?"

"Sure," Vujs said uncertainly. "In my head, sure."

"Well, why don't you run down that 'checklist' and see whether or not 'Bridge Lights' is checked off. 'Cause I'm looking right at 'em and they aren't on."

After the call, Vujs immediately disappeared underneath the spiral ramp up to the bridge, where the locked circuit breaker box is.

Vujs's goal is to have a flawless March. For one month a year, the stadium must run smoothly, perfectly. In this regard, Vujs is not unlike the ballplayers in the field: he is docked for errors, but there is no statistic recognizing his tireless efforts to ensure that bad things don't happen.

• • •

The ten light poles of Phoenix Muni support 162 lamps (as opposed to the 400 they carried at the 54,000-seat Polo Grounds), 18 of which are 400-watt security fixtures trained on the stands for pedestrian traffic, Vujs's territory. The security lamps, arranged in threes, aimed down as opposed to across and outfitted with Nema Type-6 Reflectors, look like bluebells drooping from the light poles' stems. The fixtures are mounted on ballasts that aim the lamps and control and modulate the amount of electricity flowing to each lamp.

The other 154 fixtures engage 15-megawatt (1,500,000 watts, about equivalent to the power of thirty thousand conventional lightbulbs at once) lamps, serried into banks of double-tiered seven-lamp rows on six of the eight standards. These lamps appear more confident in their arrangement, aimed across the field. The other two poles, to either side of home plate and aimed across the infield, carry three stacks of lamps, the top bank holding a row of seven, with two neatly stacked rows of six lamps below. There are eight lamp towers total mounted on the ten poles: the left- and rightfield concourse poles are joined in pairs, and the individual poles are connected together by a steel "Z" a third of the way up.

Augie Ojeda attempts his catch in shallow left-center. According to Muni's aiming diagram, this is an area beyond the exact spot where 15- megawatt lamp number 12 is aimed, a limbo when it comes to the stadium's light field. For a professional ballpark, 150–200 foot-candles is considered standard coverage, with the infield generally 20 to 30 foot-candles brighter than the outfield. The way the lights are aimed at the field is similar to the way the fielders themselves are positioned. Bloops into the shallow fields correspond to unpatrolled zones, limbos, gaps, shadows between the lights. The territories on the field that lie farthest from immediate policing are then its frontiers. The stadium's aiming diagram shows this clearly enough, an empty, uncovered space in shallow left and right, slight, barely noticeable dimples in the stadium's light surface like dark patches on the moon. The map resembles a blueprint, and the T-shaped crossing of the aimed lamps' beams in the outfield is what fielders have by way of illumination, enough to ensure that there is no Bermuda Triangle (unless the ball gets "lost in the lights," or the glare) on the field.

While Ojeda chases down the bloop, navigates the lull in the stadium's light field, I question how history slips into these dark patches, these interstices of light. Do events similarly "bloop" off the radar beyond the infield, or are they recognized immediately as "history in the making"? Or are these questions moot now? Has history left Muni altogether, left spring training behind, these light poles no longer custodians of a stage prone to history but retired, like a police officer acting as a security guard? Does it matter what happens in the dregs of lamp number 12's light? At first blush—no one on, no one out, and with "spring training" called strikes—whether Ojeda stabs the ball short of the ground with his glove seems irrelevant: there is no playoff now, not even a regular season box score at stake.

Taking a closer look, however, something *is* offered up: context. By baseball standards, Ojeda is no spring chicken: he turned thirty-two in December and has been around the big leagues. Now, his fielding must "back up" his pitcher, Jorge Julio. But, two and a half years earlier, on the night of September 7th, 2004, Julio, then the Baltimore Orioles' closer, in an act of frustration after yielding a go-ahead (and eventual game-winning) home run to Minnesota Twin Michael Cuddyer, issued a "brush back" pitch to the next hitter, who happened to be none other than a seldom-played "journeyman," a Twin utility infielder named Augie Ojeda. Julio was ejected from the game, and three days later suspended four games by Major League Baseball. Catching Julio that night was Oriole Javy Lopez, who said afterwards of the nasty pitch, which by all appearances was an attempt to bean Ojeda: "One thing I do know: if he hit him with a pitch, it would have killed him."

It would be Julio's last month as the Orioles' closer; the following year he was replaced by B. J. Ryan and demoted to middle relief. Up to that point, 2004 had been a productive season for Julio: for the year, he converted 22 of 26 save chances on a mediocre Orioles team. Now, Julio and Ojeda, after several stops each along the way, have ended up on the same squad trying together—in a coordinated (and in this case, considering Ojeda's tracking of the ball, potentially collaborative) effort—to make "the bigs" once again in March of 2007.

On the bloop, Ojeda's job is to put every ounce of energy in his body into helping Julio have one fewer base runner to face, one fewer out to earn, to preserve the perfect outing of the teammate who, two years prior, had tried to take off his head with a baseball at the distance of sixty feet, six inches. And the reality is: the thought—the memory—probably never enters Ojeda's head.

So much for history.

• • •

During the day the lights are off, of course, their lamps milky, cloudy. I sit in the rightfield bleachers away from several shouting kids tearing across the seats beneath Muni's signature concrete, accordion-roof grandstand. The poles are painted garish silver, though the upper part of some of the poles is smudged with red, rust washed down by rain from the bilevel maintenance catwalks—referred to as "baskets"—appended behind the banks of light fixtures. Blackbirds' choruses can be heard from the palo verde and mesquite trees around the stadium. Papago Park's giant red rock buttes that look as if they belong on Mars crop up, surreal, beyond the light stand-ards in the outfield. The metal bleachers tick around me like a hundred car engines just cut. Overhead, airplanes descend in their final approach to Sky Harbor. A single sparrow hops between the bleachers, scavenging.

The bases of the steel poles are riveted with huge screws around which giant hex-agonal nuts have been wound to hold them in place, clamping them to the ground. The poles are hollow and one hundred feet high. On the base is an emblem: "Union Metal MFG. Co. Canton, OHIO. U.S.A." A steel-sheathed conduit runs down the pole, encasing the electrical wiring. In the left- and rightfield bleachers are the two banks of lights each supported by two poles instead of one and rising from the con-course seats. Each of the ten poles is saddled with ballast boxes around the front; rungs extend outward from the poles to allow for maintenance work. The double poles are fused by the Z-shaped metal connection, and each of these double con-course poles is mounted with speakers. The double poles also support the netting that runs all the way behind home plate. The two leftfield poles are ringed halfway up by a circular cluster of cell phone antennae like choke collars, not uncommon on high points in small towns or cities. The leftfield and left-center poles' clusters are owned by different companies. When another company wanted to lease pole space for the right-center pole, Vujs finally drew the line and said no, as if he were done leasing out tree house space. The companies on the two leftfield poles do their work at 3 A.M., so as not to disturb any of the stadium's daytime activities.

Vujs has hired Fluoresco Lighting & Signs as the company in charge of making sure his lights are operating at full capacity come March, that not one of the 162 lamps will fail to strike. From the press box at the night game, when Vujs thinks he sees a dull lamp in the standard on the left-center pole, he frowns. But later it turns out the lamp was just aimed directly down along the warning track.

Fluoresco began in Tucson in 1961 and now maintains many stadiums, both professional and municipal, across the American West. No one at the company has climbed "the poles from New York" in a number of years, though if there's a person on earth for whom the Polo Grounds' light poles are real (perhaps too much so), it's probably Ted Frisbee. Frisbee has climbed every one of the poles at Muni, relamped the ballpark at one time, and "put on all the heads at third base and home plate."

Perhaps that's why he's a little reluctant to speak about them. For him, at bottom, it's a matter of trust.

Like most pole climbers, Frisbee is lanky, with the requisite wingspan to reach the rungs. He is in his mid-fifties with black hair slicked back, showing gray at the edges. He still has the 1970s look, and smells of cigarette smoke. His work uniform consists of a short-sleeved, pin-striped mechanic's shirt with a cursive red "Ted" stitched over his breast pocket. He is unexpectedly soft-spoken.

What Frisbee—affectionately described by Fluoresco's service manager, Tim Ocker, as the "old dog of this world"—remembers as the distinguishing characteristic of the old Polo Grounds light poles are their "double stage" catwalks. One catwalk is layered on top of the other to allow for the servicing of both tiers of lights, and there is a trapdoor between the two. He remembers he once retrofitted the poles with new fixtures. He remembers that the fixtures in the corners of the catwalk are harder to get to, especially when he was given a shorter cord. (Instead of the safety harnesses more common now, Frisbee worked simply with a belt around his waist tethered by this cord to the catwalk.) He remembers that the poles at home plate and at third still ran the original 1,500-watt quartz lamps (the rest had changed over already to metal halide), which provide a whiter light and unlike halides don't need time to warm up, firing instantly, though they are more expensive and not as durable. He remembers traversing the double poles, "going across" when he probably shouldn't have, from one to the other. He was able to complete this dangerous and tricky maneuver because, though he doesn't remember the exact span between the double poles, he has those trademark long arms and legs of a climber. ("I could do it," he says.) He remembers how, like bridges and skyscrapers, the poles would sway in the wind at the top ("with the clouds and the planes flying over you"). Being atop one of the two double poles, with the arm going across the center, seemed especially precarious when the other pole would sway, not in unison with the pole he was working on.

"You're on one and seeing kind of like this stuff . . ." he says, mimicking the swaying with a gesture, his palms facing each other and doing an out-of-rhythm rumba.

The reason he had to climb the old Polo Grounds poles was because Amtech, the company he then worked for as a full-time climber, had limited equipment: its tallest crane was fifty-five feet high. Meaning, he'd have to climb the rest of the way—forty-five feet—up to the catwalks.

He doesn't remember how many years ago it was—or the exact date— nor does he remember which pole it was, but his days as a climber ended some fifteen to twenty years ago. He stopped climbing not because he couldn't, but because he wouldn't. (He mostly shies away from ballparks now.)

He was working alone that day. It may have been in preparation for a Pink Floyd concert, which he claims is the last time he worked on the lights at Muni. (Pink Floyd only played Muni twice, April 25th and 26th of 1988; Frisbee's work was probably at least a week or so in advance of those dates.) At first, he laughs when recalling that day, before telling me why he stopped climbing. He is coy about disclosing his story, laughing as if to say, "Why the hell did I—much less anyone else—ever do that?"

"It's something you don't do all the time," he tells me. "You have to kind of get used to it again. You have to build up a little nerve."

His job that day was to turn off the breakers. There were no safety harnesses then, he reminds me, just that belt hooked to a rope he'd run from the railing of the enclosed catwalk. "I fell through the trapdoor," he says, running a hand through his slicked hair and letting it land on his shoulder blades, as if pinching them together. "I was up on the top stage. I didn't close the trapdoor and fell through to the next level. I had that so-called safety belt thing on, and that left me dangling. There's a ladder that climbs up to the next one. When I went through, I just tore up my whole side. There was nobody else out there."

He'd fallen from the top stage to the bottom—a distance of about six feet.

"But I was tied off on the top, so when I dropped down, I wasn't touching at the bottom. I had to, you know, grab hold of the ladder section of it, and . . . I had to climb all the way down. There was nobody there."

Without stricter safety standards, Frisbee says he "just wouldn't continue. . . . It was just . . . something I just said, 'No, I don't need to do this crap anymore. I don't mind doing this line of work but . . .'"

I ask him if he liked climbing. He leans back in his chair, his hands folded in his lap.

"Not necessarily. Like I said, if you do it all the time, it's one thing. You've got to trust your piece of equipment. I had no idea when I grab that rung if it ain't going to come off in my hand, you know. . . . You don't know who put it together, or what happens throughout the years. So. Back then, they didn't have a safety cable. It was just a pole and the rungs."

Now, Fluoresco's workers maintain the stadium concourse's poles using a "knuckle boom," a crane Vujs describes as moving forwards and backwards and bending and turning like an inchworm. The "boom" is a 135-foot articulating crane that allows maintenance workers to avoid obstacles—in this case, the stands, the crane positioned along the concourse. A bucket truck (containing a hoist) runs along the dirt of the warning track to maintain the outfield poles. One of the challenges the old poles present is that the ballast boxes are on the front of the poles, which makes them difficult to get to because of the pegs extending from the sides, making for a long reach. Compounding this difficulty is that the ballasts are heavy, and about the size of a pound cake. The concourse's double poles are also a challenge because the grass of the field cannot be disturbed. Vujs tells me the light poles have preserved some magic, brought some luck with them. To his eye, not one foul ball has ever hit them.

• • •

Despite the protracted demolition, six days before the first sledgehammers struck Thomson's famous fence, a small advertisement appeared in the *New York Times* from the Wrecking Corporation of America: among items available from other demolition sites ("SELLING OUT: Entire Power Plant Equipment formerly NIAGARA-MOHAWK-HERKIMER, NEW YORK STATION or RAYMOND STREET JAIL, Brooklyn, New York SELLING: Usable granite, various sizes; Fencing, gratings and other usable items") was listed "DEMOLISHING—POLO GROUNDS, Ball Park, New York City SELLING: Approximately 54,000 seats; 100—flag poles; 1—Scoreboard; 8—Tower Lights."

Avirom, the manager, had pledged to pick the Polo Grounds "clean as a bone." He said the four hundred lamps that were left in the eight steel light towers would be sold, as would the steel piping, as would the "sacred" sod (a two-square-foot section of which, from centerfield, the Giants had taken with them to San Francisco in 1957). The phone number to call was MU 2-7595.

Avirom said some seats and the Giants' bench would go to the Baseball Hall of Fame in Cooperstown, New York. He concluded that the "cats and dogs who live here will be able to take care of themselves." The light poles, on the other hand, were transported—most likely a long load by train, with the baskets, catwalks, and the lighting fixtures torn off—crosscountry to Arizona.

• • •

James Vujs is constantly minimizing hazards and risk; concourse minutiae are his areas of expertise. He controls placement and forces movement all over the stadium floor. Since he works hand-in-hand with the A's spring training staff, some of whom are directly involved with the corporate sponsors, occasionally he can make the staff members look good by playing the role of the bad guy. This good cop/bad cop routine—removing corporate bigwigs from places on his property where they aren't allowed—seems to be one aspect of the job Vujs enjoys. A spring training sponsor's tent support pole is precariously close to the queue at the concession stands, and Vujs delegates one of his men to have the tent moved. Another sponsor's table is clogging pedestrian traffic at the gate; Vujs instructs them to relocate.

Tonight, the biggest sponsor is an ABC *Dancing with the Stars* promotion. Models in purple bikinis and sheer, gauzy, tutulike outfits are traipsing around the concourse accompanied by ridiculous-looking mascots dressed in giant gold star costumes. They create a regal entourage of gold and purple and seem to think they can go wherever they want. First, Vujs and I see them down on the field. During the game, the girls are posing with men from the crowd on top of the dugouts. I find myself hoping the entourage does something wrong to provoke Vujs's "bad cop" routine, to see Vujs mano a mano with the "stars," but apparently in his view their grandstanding is okay.

Power cords are another potential problem for Vujs. Many of the sponsors' tables require power, and Vujs is in charge of making sure the cords are laid so as to avoid any potential injuries to the stadium's guests. His trick is to run the cords along the bases of walls and in the seams of the concrete, covered with silver duct tape. These are security measures, more ways of minimizing risk and increasing safety, of preventing accidents from happening.

He tells me all of this as we stand under the concourse's double light pole along the rightfield foul line. He is showing me how he has run the power cords along the shortest distance possible while at the same time minimizing risk down the handicap walkway ramp from the seats. Above us the power running through the lights makes a droning sound, a lower-pitched, sustained version of the sound a fly makes when it buzzes in your ear.

When shadows cross the infield, an hour or so before sunset, the lights are turned on via two switches—one for the light poles on each side of the field—back behind the scoreboard in centerfield. Muni's lamps are metal halide (HID) and require about ten minutes to fully kindle, the way streetlights begin dim and then take time to warm up.

Once, Vujs had shut down the lights for a fireworks display beyond the outfield during the seventh-inning stretch. When the show was over, the lights didn't rekindle immediately. For ten minutes the stadium remained in darkness, the slow halide lamps glowing like dim moons. For this reason, many stadiums now have both HID and quartz fixtures, the former taking time to kindle, the latter striking immediately.

● ● ●

The lamps at Muni are outfitted with glare shields, visors, and dampeners for every one of the 162 lamps. The lamps look a little like they have on ball caps, the Nema-type reflector a bill extended out over the light. The more precision with which the lights are aimed, the less glare: Muni's lamps have advanced directional accoutrements. The lighting system was devised by Musco Lighting in Oskaloosa, Iowa. The old-fashioned way to aim lights was at night, with before and after readings taken on the field to ensure proper coverage.

But now, says Gary Gryder, Fluoresco's vice president of corporate sales and marketing, the process of re-aiming the lights, which happens almost every year, has become a little more high-tech:

"Generally there is a red dot that's on the fixture itself right in the middle where there's an aiming spot, and you can only see it when it's aimed properly. So you stand on the field with a pair of binoculars and the guy [on the pole] just kind of moves it around until you can see it. And then you tell him it's good, and you tighten it down."

This seems right—that a person standing on the field would need binoculars to make sure that the lamps were aimed right, that the spaces illuminated by looking back, by history, would have to be precisely aimed, dependent on some strange red spot, some glimmer, in the full glare of 1,500,000-watt metal halide lamps. It's no small wonder that the guy on the field doesn't go blind, and then I wonder about historians—all that looking back. The person doesn't even need to be a historian; someone merely nostalgic would do. Gravity tamps down the ball's flights, the Polo Grounds is demolished, but the nostalgically inclined person—and there are many—keeps propping those balls back up into the air, remembering

Mays's "Catch" and Thomson's "Shot," buoying the balls and refusing to let them touch the ground. And I think to myself, for a fleeting second, *this* is what these light poles are about, if only for a moment: once upon a time they brought light to one of baseball's great stages. Occasionally, they stood in for the sun.

● ● ●

Augie Ojeda is quick enough to get under the bloop fly. He keeps the mitt close to his chest; he knows he won't have to reach. The cognitive ability allowing a fielder to track a ball, an instinctual gauge for distance and trajectory that might even be faster than a computer and can trace the arc of a ball in its first inches off the bat, this combination of knowledge and acumen gathered from tracking hundreds of fly balls, blended with this instant analysis of the ball's trajectory and how to avoid the glare of the stadium lights—*this* is what Augie Ojeda has going for him.

Maybe that's what allows him, scurrying out to shallow left, to make "the catch." Open mitt against chest, the ball drops in barely over his shoulder, a basket catch before he flops to the ground from the effort of his run.

Don Delillo's epic, *Underworld* (1996), recalls the Polo Grounds' other famous moment, "the Shot," using Thomson's home run ball as its central structural motif. This is a place where the Polo Grounds remains standing, one could argue. The novel's first forty-nine pages are devoted to Cotter Martin's retrieval of the ball that fateful afternoon. Delillo writes, "[Martin] hears the crescendoing last chords of the national anthem and sees the great open horseshoe of the grandstand and that unfolding vision of the grass that always seems to mean he has stepped outside his life. . . . It is the excitement of a revealed thing."

I think about the things I idealize, my flights of fancy, how my imagination occasionally makes somethings out of nothings. How I often willfully dream, instead of letting dreams come to me; how I prefer them that way.

• • •

One gameless night, the lights are on, though no one is home. They can be seen blazing from the 202 Loop Freeway, at first clearly visible and then spotted through the horizon-scrapers of a new Tempe office park. From a greater distance, they can be seen merely as a small dome of light rising from the desert, pushing up from the ground to the sky. There is the stadium, deserted, light banks bright, as hard to look at as eight distinct (and halide) suns; the field is green, Bermuda grass viridescent like a lime green highlighter. There is no sound but a leaf blower, one of Vujs's men (by several degrees of separation; the man is actually hired out by contract) tidying up the parking lot from the day game.

I'm reminded of pictures I've seen on the Internet of the Polo Grounds' light standards in their original positions, perched on the green wraparound grandstand of the park. Roger Angell wrote of entering the Polo Grounds: "You came slowly down the John T. Brush [the Giants' original owner in the 1910s] stairs to the cool of the evening, looking down at the flags and the tiers of brilliant floodlights on the stands and, beyond them, at the softer shimmer of lights on the Harlem River." I think of the pictures posted on the Internet of the lights, the poles decorated with some four hundred smaller lamps, tiered on four horizontal shelves, looking, from a distance, like birds ranked on power lines against the sky or, up close, a dizzying wind chime collection.

There are entire online communities devoted to discussion of the old Polo Grounds. The physical site in Manhattan has long since been converted into four thirty-floor apartment buildings that accommodate 1,614 families. A Willie Mays playground, a pool of asphalt featuring four basketball backboards, occupies the place where centerfield once was.

When the last major league baseball game was played at the Polo Grounds on September 18, 1963, only 1,752 fans gathered to watch the Mets, the lowest draw the Mets had had in their two years of existence. The Jets played football at the Polo Grounds until December 14, 1963, their last game there a 19-10 loss to the Bills. (The old stadium's football history, though less storied, offers several memorable moments: the appearance of the Bears' Red Grange in 1924 that put professional football on the map and the famous Giants-Bears sneaker game in 1935 when the

Giants changed their cleats at halftime because of the muddy turf and dominated the second half.)

The Mets moved the following season from the Polo Grounds to Shea Stadium in Flushing Meadows. Their first night game was greeted the next day in the *Times* with the headline "Shea's Lights Make Brilliant Debut." Comments from fans ranged from "Everything just seems to be clearer" to "It makes the game more interesting" to "Best light I've ever seen" to "It's definitely the brightest park in the majors." The players complained, saying they couldn't look directly into the lights but had to turn their heads. Mets shortstop Al Moran said, "There's a little bit of a bluish glare . . . and I imagine we'll have an advantage when we get used to it." The "new" light came from a "circular necklace" of 884 mercury-vapor lamps blended with 820 incandescent quartz lamps to avoid a "blue-out." Moran concluded, "There are no shadows at all. . . . It's so clear, you can see an ant crawling across the grass." (Shea Stadium will be replaced as the Mets' home by Citi Field for Opening Day, 2009.)

But members of the online community, particularly members of baseball-fever. com and its forums immersed in the nitty-gritty specifics (a form of nostalgic rigor, perhaps), remain more interested in Polo Grounds' baseball. One discussion debates whether, after the $250,000 1962 renovation before the Mets (temporarily) moved in, the grandstand was repainted green or painted blue. The posts go back and forth on the subject, old men debating the vividness of their memories in relative anonymity. The last post, written on January 17, 2007, at 9:25 P.M. by someone with the screen name Elvis, underneath which his sig says, "That's the way it is"—the post that put the issue to bed, so to speak—reads: "I believe that the Polo Grounds was indeed repainted in the early '60s, but that the 'ballpark green' wasn't replaced by blue, but rather this color, which is a more bluish-green, but still more green than blue."

● ● ●

In 1982, the Giants relocated their spring training to Scottsdale, and the lights remained behind when the A's took over the stadium. The lamps are seldom used, less than five hundred hours a year; the stadium, once spring training is over, remains mostly idle through the year's other eleven months, a lengthy, inningless off-season. When Muni was built in 1964, the sports editor of the *Arizona Republic* called it a "million dollar grass farm."

By June, when I look down on the stadium from a plane, desert dust has overrun Muni's seats down each foul line, nature's attempt to lay claim to the stadium's land. Only the seats under the accordion-roofed grandstand remain distinctly blue, sheltered from the wind. The practice facility directly adjacent to Muni—another identical diamond with identical outfield grass and dimensions—gives the cluster the appearance of houses or hotels piling up on the same property in Monopoly: the new Arizona Avenue.

The D-backs placed Jorge Julio on waivers the last week of spring training. He was picked up by the Marlins, where he registered an ERA over 10 before being traded to the Colorado Rockies, where, at the halfway point of the season, he has enjoyed some success. (ESPN.com blogger Nate Ravitz unsympathetically describes Julio's resurgence as "like a scab that keeps growing back.")

By the 2007 All-Star break, Augie Ojeda has been back in the bigs for a month. For his entire career since he was drafted by the Orioles in the thirteenth round of the 1996 amateur draft (only four of the thirty players selected in that draft stanza ever played in a big league game), he has shuttled between the minors and the majors. Entering the season, he had appeared in 178 career big league games—just over one complete season's worth in eleven years of professional baseball. But this season things are looking up. He goes into the break with a .382 batting average that has raised his career average to .232. Of his 13 hits in 34 major league at bats this season, one was his sixth career home run.

Ojeda has even gained a reputation. The scribes who refer to themselves online as the "Diamondhacks" have this to say about Ojeda: "If Honus Wagner had a 'Mini-me,' this guy is it." And Ojeda has made his spectacular over-the-shoulder catches routine. On MLB.com, his list of highlights from the regular season includes an "over the shoulder" video download.

The catch comes from a June 23rd home interleague game against—you guessed it—the Baltimore Orioles (the team that drafted him, nearly killed him, and against which he practically patents his spectacular play). There is one out, a man on third. Clad in the D-backs' new black shirt, Ojeda—retaining number 11—tracks a bloop over his shoulder. The bloop slices sharply, and Ojeda bends with the ball. He makes the catch, his legs sliding out from under him. He jumps up and—like the immortal Mays highlight—fires the ball back to hold any runners.

Jake Young is from Los Angeles, California, and has studied writing at Princeton and Arizona State Universities. He is currently at work on a novel.

THE BASEBALL PASTORAL

Jeff Greenfield

Over the years, working as a commentator and political analyst for ABC, CNN, PBS, and now CBS, Jeff Greenfield has reported on baseball stories, interviewing the likes of Hank Aaron and baseball commissioner Bud Selig. In the stands, however, he abandons journalistic impartiality, and is, this essay makes clear, a born and bred Yankees fan. [L. G.]

There's a scene in *City Slickers* where Billy Crystal, in the midst of the midlife crisis that has taken him out West, recalls with near-reverence his first visit to Yankee Stadium: his first glimpse of the field as he and his father emerge from the tunnel, the brilliant blue sky, the blinding white of the uniforms, the rich green grass.

That scene hit me with special force, because I had written almost exactly the same scene in a widely unread book I'd published nearly twenty years before *City Slickers* hit the screens. Plagiarism? Hardly. Coincidence? Much more than that. If my friends and contemporaries are any clue, this is something close to a collective memory as pervasive and as powerful as a memory of a first love, or first glimpse of Paris at night. It is so powerful, in fact, that it survives the most earnest, heartfelt, painful efforts of the belles-lettres crowd to pound the game over the head with Meaning.

I've had my own innings at infusing Great Thoughts; decades ago I proudly concluded that the reason baseball was the classic American pas time was that it paid joint homage to our two historic eras: the outfield, unbounded by the strict dimensions that apply to other sports, was our tribute to our agricultural roots. The batting order and method of scoring, on the other hand, were rigidly linear; unlike any other sport's players, batters had to proceed in exact order, and the movement around the bases was modeled on the assembly line, and thus, this aspect of the game saluted our industrial era.

I know, I know. At least I have the solace of knowing I am not alone in my ventures into the portentous: I've seen otherwise admirable writers produce enough hot air to melt the polar ice caps with talk of "the agora" and the mythological dimensions of players past—a tendency Philip Roth not-so-subtly skewered in *The Great American Novel,* his account of the nonexistent Patriot League of the 1940s, in which he named his characters, such as Gil Gamesh and Tris Mesgistus, after mythic figures.

I now define the game's hold on me in more personal, less cosmic terms. At its simplest, many of my most powerful memories are rooted in the ballpark. And the reason may be laughably simple: I can trace those memories back further than almost any other part of my life. And, with just a couple of exceptions, they are memories of the *same* ballpark.

My father first took me to Yankee Stadium when I was five years old, well over half a century ago. It was a game against the St. Louis Browns, a game so bizarre the late sportswriter Tom Meany once chronicled it as one of the weirdest he'd never seen. The final score was 20-2. All *three* Yankee catchers—Yogi Berra, Charlie Silvera, and future manager Ralph Houk—were beaned by opposing pitchers. (I believe outfielder Hank Bauer wound up as the final catcher, but I could be wrong). I'm pretty sure Joe DiMaggio hit a bases-loaded ground-rule double into the bleachers. I *know* my father kept telling me, "You know, this isn't really like most baseball games."

For the next several years, trips to the Stadium became a regular father-son outing, always following the same ritual. My father was a highly punctual man, and back in the 1950s, there were far more general admission seats than there are now, so an early arrival meant a choice of excellent upper-deck seats behind home plate.

We sometimes arrived at the Stadium as the grounds crew was setting up the cage for batting practice, which was fine with us; it left plenty of time for me to memorize the statistics that filled the sports pages of the Sunday *New York Times*, while devouring the tunaon-white sandwiches my mother had prepared. (On a warm summer day the oil slick that formed on the brown paper bag was enough to chill the heart of any self-respecting environmentalist.)

My father was a good and kind man, but like most men of his time, was not comfortable sharing his feelings, and I'm pretty sure I would have found any effort on his part more than a little strange. But we talked a lot of baseball on those Sunday afternoons. He was a passionate Brooklyn Dodgers fan, probably because he'd spent a lot of his childhood in Brooklyn, and his parents owned a candy store near Ebbets Field, where some of the Dodgers used to drop in on their way to work. (I don't know how many times he told me about the day Pee Wee Reese, off to join the navy in World War II, bought enough "good luck" candy bars to get him through the war. Apparently they did the trick.) So we'd argue the merits of Reese versus Rizzuto, Berra versus Campanella, even Duke Snider versus DiMaggio.

And even when World Series time came around, we'd wind up at the Stadium, if only in the bleachers. I don't know how hard it was to get tickets in those days, but I knew he was determined to get us in the ballpark. They may not have been the best seats in the house, but we were there for the fifth game of the 1953 World Series, an incredible eleven-inning 6-5 Dodger victory highlighted by spectacular late-inning, home-run-saving catches by Dodger outfielders.

Over the years, the memories of these games, and of the games I attended with my friends when I grew old enough, formed as solid a core of my past as any experiences I ever had. No matter how long ago they were, they come back to me every time I'm at the Stadium. For instance, there has not been a game in the last forty years when I haven't looked out to rightfield, where the tiara-like façade used to be, and remembered a 1956 game when Mickey Mantle hit a ball that kept rising, and rising—until a cheer from the fans in rightfield, like nothing I have heard before or since, exploded throughout the park. The ball had hit a mere eighteen inches below the top of the roof—the closest any player has ever come to hitting a fair ball out of the park during a ball game. (This was the first game Billy Crystal ever attended, a story he tells in his brilliant one-man show, "700 Sundays." When I met Crystal backstage, I remembered that I'd saved the scorecard from that game for thirty years; I'm still sorry I threw it out. On the other hand, I'm glad I stopped keeping score somewhere in my middle forties; you get to see a lot more of the game when you're not noting down the hieroglyphics required for accurate record-keeping.)

When my children came along, the memories grew to stretch back and forth across the generations. When my daughter Casey was about nine, I got three tickets to a box seat next to the visiting team's dugout, and brought Casey and my father to the game. When the three of us walked out of the tunnel into the stands, I found myself close to tears. A few minutes later, I was struck by less pleasant memories when my father, who has always believed in Behaving the Right Way, became progressively more annoyed by the young fans crowding the railing in front of him looking for autographs or baseballs, even though the game was about an hour away from starting. (The apple doesn't fall far from the tree; to this day, I channel his spirit when the yahoos in front of me decide to jump up every time a Yankee pitcher gets two strikes on the opposing batter.)

My son, David, came into sports-fanhood in the late 1980s and early '90s, when both the Yankees and the Mets were struggling. Basketball was his passion—we'll pass over his blessedly brief flirtation with pro wrestling, except to note that my paternal devotion was such that I took him, in person, to two WWF events at Madison Square Garden, and planned to tell anyone who recognized me that we were on our way to a porn store. Baseball, for Dave, was too slow, too stately.

And then something happened: maybe it was the onset of wisdom. Maybe it was that the Yankees began to win. But suddenly, he became a fan; and by the time he was ten, he'd learned to appreciate not just the game, but also its history. When he'd swing a bat in our yard on weekends, my job—apart from pitching to him—was to announce the lineup of major league All-Stars, past and present. I knew the history had taken when he

began to ape the distinctive swing of Stan Musial, or reenact Babe Ruth's "I'm calling my shot" gesture from the 1932 World Series.

In our years at the Stadium, Dave and I have collected more than our share of memories. In 2001, we were part of the dispirited crowd that was preparing to leave in anticipation of a devastating Game Four loss to the Arizona Diamondbacks. The Yankees were two runs down with two out in the ninth and a runner on first. We had put on our coats, but Dave had long since become a firm adherent of the game-ain't-over-till-the-last-man's-out school of thought. When Tino Martinez slammed a game-tying homer off reliever Byung-Hyun Kim, the roar of the crowd was otherworldly; when Derek Jeter won the game with a two-out homer in the tenth, I told Dave he'd likely never experience anything so dramatic ever again. And my prediction held true: for twenty-four hours. The next night, the Yankees were two runs down with two out in the ninth, and a runner on second.

"Put on your coat, Dave," I said.

"We're not leaving," he said.

"No, of course not, but if you put on your coat, Brosius'll tie the game up with a homer."

We did—and he did. As much as I remember the sound of Yankee Stadium slowly leaving the gravitational pull of the earth, I also wanted Dave to see reliever Byung-Hyun Kim on the mound, sinking to his knees in utter despair. When you're in the midst of exultation, it's good to remember someone else is in pain.

We learned that lesson well—not just when Arizona won the next two games and the Series back in Phoenix, but in the coming years. In 2002, I paid an extortionate amount of money so Dave and I could attend Game Six of the Series against the Florida Marlins. Inning after inning, as young Josh Beckett shut the Yankees down, the fans began cheering again, certain that the magic of 2001 would repeat. When the game—and the Series—finally ended, after a masterful shutout, the silence was as profound as any sound I've ever heard.

Two years later, we were in the best seats in the house—the gift of a very well-connected sports figure—for Game Seven of the American League Championship Series. Surely God would not let the Boston Red Sox fall behind three games to none, and then actually *win*. Dave and I swapped tales of the great Sox foldos of the past: Enos Slaughter's trip around the bases in 1946, Bucky Bleeping Dent's home run in the '78 playoffs, Buckner's bobble of a Mookie Wilson ground ball at Shea in '86, Pedro's collapse in '03. Heck, we'd been at that classic twelve-inning Red Sox–Yankees game in July, when Derek Jeter had flown head first into the stands to catch a critical short fly ball.

Our euphoria lasted all the way into the top half of the first inning, when David Ortiz hit a two-run homer with two outs. An inning later, with the bases loaded,

Johnny Damon stepped up to the plate. From our splendid seats in the first row just behind home plate, I remember watching Kevin Brown let the pitch go and muttering, "look out!" just before Damon hit the grand-slam home run that effectively ended the game, giving us a fine seat for the longest funeral in Yankee Stadium history.

And in a funny way, I'm as happy Dave and I were witnesses to the losses as I am that we saw those incredible back-to-back comebacks in 2001. It doesn't require any pompous fatherly instructions to figure out what you take away from games like those.

Those trips to the Stadium bond us in ways the scoreboard doesn't report. Dave is something of a sports polymath, and I get a kick out of watching him engage other fans in conversation. When he overhears fans exchanging massive amounts of blatant misinformation, there is a glint in his eye as he stores the howlers away for later examination. He even indulges my memories of Mantle and Berra, and Vic Raschi and Allie Reynolds—up to a point. And there are times when I've brought Dave along on reporting gigs for ABC and now CNN, not just because I thought he'd get a kick out of being on the field, but because he's simply better than I am at recognizing the players I might want to interview.

And on my office wall is a picture, more than twenty years old, of a summer softball group I'm part of that got to play a softball game at Yankee Stadium, thanks to Tom Brokaw. Dave is on my shoulders, and I'm getting ready to play in my first and last Stadium appearance. I dribbled a soft ground ball down the third-base line, and beat the throw to first. As I tell it, I have a 1.000 batting average at the Stadium, and if my listeners imagine me slamming a ball into the power alley—shades of Jerry Coleman winning the pennant against the Red Sox in 1949—I am not about to disabuse them.

Jeff Greenfield is a senior political correspondent at CBS, host of PBS's *CEO Exchange,* and the author of a dozen books.

ON THE BALL

Roger Angell

Roger Angell began writing about baseball in 1962, when New Yorker editor William Shawn sent him to Florida to cover spring training. He still writes about baseball for the magazine and has been called "the poet laureate of baseball" and "the best baseball writer ever." As to why baseball is the subject of so much writing, Angell speculated, in a 2003 interview with Robert Birnbaum, that "most of the sports that get lengthy books written about them are fairly lengthy themselves.... And God knows there is a lot of time in baseball. You can sit there and take notes and watch the field and have an idea once in a while." [L. G.]

Summer 1976

It weighs just over five ounces and measures between 2.86 and 2.94 inches in diameter. It is made of a composition-cork nucleus encased in two thin layers of rubber, one black and one red, surrounded by 121 yards of tightly wrapped blue-gray wool yarn, 45 yards of white wool yarn, 53 more yards of blue-gray wool yarn, 150 yards of fine cotton yarn, a coat of rubber cement, and a cowhide (formerly horsehide) exterior, which is held together with 216 slightly raised red cotton stitches. Printed certifications, endorsements, and outdoor advertising spherically attest to its authenticity. Like most institutions, it is considered inferior in its present form to its ancient archetypes, and in this case the complaint is probably justified;

on occasion in recent years it has actually been known to come apart under the demands of its brief but rigorous active career. Baseballs are assembled and hand-stitched in Taiwan (before this year the work was done in Haiti, and before 1973 in Chicopee, Massachusetts), and contemporary pitchers claim that there is a tangible variation in the size and feel of the balls that now come into play in a single game; a true peewee is treasured by hurlers, and its departure from the premises, by fair means or foul, is secretly mourned. But never mind: any baseball is beautiful. No other small package comes as close to the ideal in design and utility. It is a perfect object for a man's hand. Pick it up and it instantly suggests its purpose; it is meant to be thrown a considerable distance—thrown hard and with precision. Its feel and heft are the beginning of the sport's critical dimensions; if it were a fraction of an inch larger or smaller, a few centigrams heavier or lighter, the game of baseball would be utterly different. Hold a baseball in your hand. As it happens, this one is not brand-new. Here, just to one side of the curved surgical welt of stitches, there is a pale-green grass smudge, darkening on one edge almost to black—the mark of an old infield play, a tough grounder now lost in memory. Feel the ball, turn it over in your hand; hold it across the seam or the other way, with the seam just to the side of your middle finger. Speculation stirs. You want to get outdoors and throw this spare and sensual object to somebody or, at the very least, watch somebody else throw it. The game has begun.

Thinking about the ball and its attributes seems to refresh our appreciation of this game. A couple of years ago, I began to wonder why it was that pitchers, taken as a group, seemed to be so much livelier and more garrulous than hitters. I considered the possibility of some obscure physiological linkage (the discobologlottal syndrome) and the more obvious occupational discrepancies (pitchers have a lot more spare time than other players), but then it came to me that a pitcher is the only man in baseball who can properly look on the ball as being his instrument, his accomplice. He is the only player who is granted the privilege of making offensive plans, and once the game begins he is (in concert with his catcher) the only man on the field who knows what is meant to happen next. Everything in baseball begins with the pitch, and every other part of the game—hitting, fielding, and throwing—is reflexive and defensive. (The hitters on a ball team are referred to as the "offense," but almost three-quarters of the time this is an absolute misnomer.) The batter tapping the dirt off his spikes and now stepping into the box looks sour and glum, and who can blame him, for the ball has somehow been granted in perpetuity to the wrong people. It is already an object of suspicion and hatred, and the reflex that allows him occasionally to deflect that tiny onrushing dot with his bat, and sometimes even to relaunch it violently in the opposite direction, is such a miraculous response of eye and body as to remain virtually inexplicable, even to him. There are a few dugout flannelmouths (Ted Williams, Harry Walker, Pete Rose) who can talk convincingly about the art of hitting, but, like most arts, it does not in the end seem communicable. Pitching is different. It is a craft ("the crafty portsider . . .") and is thus within reach.

The smiling pitcher begins not only with the advantage of holding his fate in his own hands, or hand, but with the knowledge that every advantage of physics and psychology seems to be on his side. A great number of surprising and unpleasant things can be done to the ball as it is delivered from the grasp of a two-hundred-pound optimist, and the first of these is simply to transform it into a projectile. Most pitchers seem hesitant to say so, but if you press them a little they will admit that the prime ingredient in their intense personal struggle with the batter is probably fear. A few pitchers in the majors have thrived without a real fastball—junk men like Eddie Lopat and Mike Cuellar, superior control artists like Bobby Shantz and Randy Jones, knuckleballers like Hoyt Wilhelm and Charlie Hough—but almost everyone else has had to hump up and throw at least an occasional no-nonsense hard one, which crosses the plate at eighty-five miles per hour, or better, and thus causes the hitter to—well, to *think* a little. The fastball sets up all the other pitches in the hurler's repertoire—the curve, the slider, the sinker, and so on—but its other purpose is to intimidate. Great fastballers like Bob Gibson, Jim Bunning, Sandy Koufax, and Nolan Ryan have always run up high strikeout figures because their money pitch was almost untouchable, but their deeper measures of success—twenty-victory seasons and low earned run averages—were due to the fact that none of the hitters they faced, not even the best of them, was immune to the thought of what a ninety-mph missile could do to a man if it struck him. They had been ever so slightly distracted, and distraction is bad for hitting. The intention of the pitcher has almost nothing to do with this; very few pitches are delivered with intent to maim. The bad dream, however, will not go away. Walter Johnson, the greatest fireballer of them all, had almost absolute control, but he is said to have worried constantly about what might happen if one of his pitches got away from him. Good hitters know all this and resolutely don't think about it (a good hitter is a man who can keep his back foot firmly planted in the box even while the rest of him is pulling back or bailing out on an inside fastball), but even these icy customers are less settled in their minds than they would like to be, just because the man out there on the mound is hiding that cannon behind his hip. Hitters, of course, do not call this fear. The word is "respect."

It should not be inferred, of course, that major-league pitchers are wholly averse to hitting batters, or *almost* hitting batters. A fastball up around the Adam's apple not only is a first-class distracter, as noted, but also discourages a hitter from habitually leaning forward in order to put more of his bat on a dipping curve or a slider over the outer rim of the plate. The truth of the matter is that pitchers and batters are engaged in a permanent private duel over their property rights to the plate, and a tough, proud hurler who senses that the man now in the batter's box has recently had the better of things will often respond in the most direct manner possible, with a hummer to the ribs. Allie Reynolds, Sal Maglie, Don Drysdale, Early Wynn, and

Bob Gibson were cold-eyed lawmen of this stripe, and the practice has by no means vanished, in spite of strictures and deplorings from the high chambers of baseball. Early this year, Lynn McGlothen, of the Cards, routinely plunked the Mets' Del Unser, who had lately been feasting on his pitches, and then violated the ancient protocol in these matters by admitting intent. Dock Ellis, now a Yankee but then a Pirate, decided early in the 1974 season that the Cincinnati Reds had somehow established dominance over his club, and he determined to set things right in his own way. (This incident is described at length in a lively new baseball book, *Dock Ellis in the Country of Baseball,* by Donald Hall.) The first Cincinnati batter of the game was Pete Rose, and the first pitch from Ellis was at his head—"not actually to *hit* him," Ellis said later, but as a "*message* to let him know that he was going to be hit." He then hit Rose in the side. The next pitch hit the next Red batter, Joe Morgan, in the kidney. The third batter was Dan Driessen, who took Ellis's second pitch in the back. With the bases loaded, Dock now threw four pitches at Tony Perez (one behind his back), but missed with all of them, walking in a run. He then missed Johnny Bench (and the plate) twice, whereupon Pirate manager Danny Murtaugh came out to the mound, stared at Ellis with silent surmise, and beckoned for a new pitcher.

Hitters can accept this sort of fugue, even if they don't exactly enjoy it, but what they do admittedly detest is a young and scatter-armed smoke-thrower, the true wild man. One famous aborigine was Steve Dalkowski, an Oriole farmhand of the late 1950s and early '60s who set records for strikeouts and jumpy batters wherever he played. In one typical stay with a Class D league, he threw 121 strikeouts and gave up 129 walks and 39 wild pitches, all in the span of 62 innings. Dalkowski never made it to the majors, but, being a legend, he is secure for the ages. "Once I saw him work a game in the Appalachian League," a gravel-voiced retired coach said to me not long ago, "and nothing was hit *forward* for seven innings—not even a foul ball." An attempt was once made to clock Dalkowski on a recording device, but his eventual mark of 93.5 mph was discounted, since he threw for forty minutes before steering a pitch into the machine's recording zone.

Better-known names in these annals of anxiety are Rex Barney, a briefly flaring Brooklyn nova of the 1940s, who once threw a no-hit game but eventually walked and wild-pitched his way out of baseball; Ryne Duren, the extremely fast and extremely nearsighted reliever for the Yankees and other American League clubs in the '50s and

'60s, whose traditional initial warm-up pitch on his being summoned to the mound was a twelve-foothigh fastball to the foul screen; and a pair of rookies named Sandy Koufax and Bob Feller. Koufax, to be sure, eventually became a superb control artist, but it took him seven years before he got his great stuff entirely together, and there were times when it seemed certain that he would be known only as another Rex Barney. Sandy recalls that when he first brought his boyish assortment of fiery sailers and bouncing rockets to spring-training camp he had difficulty getting in any mound work, because whenever he picked up his glove all the available catchers would suddenly remember pressing appointments in some distant part of the compound. Feller had almost a career-long struggle with *his* control, and four times managed to lead his league simultaneously in walks and in strikeouts. His first appearance against another major-league club came in an exhibition game against the Cardinals in the summer of 1936, when he was seventeen years old; he entered the game in the fourth inning, and eventually struck out eight batters in three innings, but when his searing fastball missed the plate it had the batters jumping around in the box like roasting popcorn. Frank Frisch, the St. Louis player-manager, carefully observed Feller's first three or four deliveries and then walked down to the end of the dugout, picked up a pencil, and removed himself from the Cardinal lineup.

• • •

The chronically depressed outlook of major-league batters was pushed to the edge of paranoia in the 1950s by the sudden and utterly unexpected arrival of the slider, or the Pitcher's Friend. The slider is an easy pitch to throw and a hard one to hit. It is delivered with the same motion as the fastball, but with the pitcher's wrist rotated approximately ninety degrees (to the right for a righthander, to the left for a southpaw), which has the effect of placing the delivering forefinger and middle finger slightly off center on the ball. The positions of hand, wrist, and arm are almost identical with those that produce a good spiral forward pass with a football. The result is an apparent three-quarter-speed fastball that suddenly changes its mind and direction. It doesn't break much—in its early days it was slightingly known as the "nickel curve"—but a couple of inches of lateral movement at the plateward end of the ball's brief sixty-foot-six-inch journey can make for an epidemic of pop-ups, foul balls, and harmless grounders. "Epidemic" is not an exaggeration. The slider was the prime agent responsible for the sickening and decline of major-league batting averages in the two decades after the Second World War, which culminated in a combined average of .237 for the two leagues in 1968. A subsequent crash program of immunization and prevention by the authorities produced from the laboratory a smaller strike zone and a lowering of the pitcher's mound by five inches, but the hitters, while saved from extermination, have never regained their state of rosy-cheeked, pre-slider good health.

For me, the true mystery of the slider is not its flight path but the circumstances of its discovery. Professional baseball got under way in the 1870s, and during all the ensuing summers uncounted thousands of young would-be Mathewsons and Seavers spent their afternoons flinging the ball in every conceivable fashion as they searched for magic fadeaways and flutter balls that would take them to Cooperstown. Why did eighty years pass before anybody noticed that a slight cocking of the wrist would be sufficient to usher in the pitchers' Golden Age? Where were Tom Swift and Frank Merriwell? What happened to American Know-How? This is almost a national disgrace. The mystery is deepened by the fact that—to my knowledge, at least—no particular pitcher or pitching coach is given credit for the discovery and propagation of the slider. Bob Lemon, who may be the first man to have pitched his way into the Hall of Fame with a slider, says he learned the pitch from Mel Harder, who was an elder mound statesman with the Indians when Lemon came up to that club, in 1946. I have also heard some old-timers say that George Blaeholder was throwing a pretty fair slider for the St. Louis Browns way back in the 1920s. But none of these worthies ever claimed to be the Johnny Appleseed of the pitch. The thing seemed to generate itself—a weed in the bull pen which overran the field. The slider has made baseball more difficult for the fan as well as for the batter. Since its action is late and minimal, and since its delivery does not require the easily recognizable arm-snap by the pitcher that heralds the true curve, the slider can be spotted only by an attentive spectator seated very close to home plate. A curve thrown by famous old pretzel-benders like Tommy Bridges and Sal Maglie really used to *curve;* you could see the thing break even if you were way out in the top deck of Section 31. Most fans, however, do not admit the loss. The contemporary bleacher critic, having watched a doll-size distant slugger swing mightily and tap the ball down to second on four bounces, smiles and enters the out in his scorecard. "Slider," he announces, and everybody nods wisely in agreement.

● ● ●

The mystery of the knuckleball is ancient and honored. Its practitioners cheerfully admit that they do not understand why the pitch behaves the way it does; nor do they know, or care much, which particular lepidopteran path it will follow on its way past the batter's infuriated swipe. They merely prop the ball on their fingertips (not, in actual fact, on the knuckles) and launch it more or less in the fashion of a paper airplane, and then, most of the time, finish the delivery with a faceward motion of the glove, thus hiding a grin. Now science has confirmed the phenomenon. Writing in *The American Journal of Physics,* Eric Sawyer and Robert G. Watts, of Tulane University, recently reported that wind-tunnel tests showed that a slowly spinning baseball is subject to forces capable of making it swerve a foot or more between the pitcher's mound and the plate. The secret, they say, appears to be the raised seams of the ball, which cause a "roughness pattern" and an uneven flow of air, resulting in a "nonsymmetric lateral force distribution and . . . a net force in one direction or another."

Like many other backyard baseball stars, I have taught myself to throw a knuckleball that moves with so little rotation that one can almost pick out the signature of Charles S. Feeney in midair; the pitch, however, has shown disappointingly few symptoms of last-minute fluttering and has so far proved to be wonderfully catchable or hittable, mostly by my wife. Now, at last, I understand the problem. In their researches, Sawyer and Watts learned that an entirely spinless knuckler is *not* subject to varying forces, and thus does not dive or veer. The ideal knuckler, they say, completes about a quarter of a revolution on its way to the plate. The speed of the pitch, moreover, is not critical, because "the magnitude of the lateral force increases approximately as the square of the velocity," which means that the total lateral movement is "independent of the speed of the pitch."

All this has been perfectly understood (if less politely defined) by any catcher who has been the battery mate of a star knuckleballer, and has thus spent six or seven innings groveling in the dirt in imitation of a bulldog cornering a nest of field mice. Modern catchers have the assistance of outsized gloves (which lately have begun

to approach the diameter of tea trays), and so enjoy a considerable advantage over some of their ancient predecessors in capturing the knuckler. In the middle 1940s, the receivers for the Washington Senators had to deal with a pitching staff that included *four* knuckleball specialists—Dutch Leonard, Johnny Niggeling, Mickey Haefner, and Roger Wolff. Among the ill-equipped Washington catchers who tried to fend off almost daily mid-afternoon clouds of deranged butterflies were Rick Ferrell and Jake Early; Early eventually was called up to serve in the armed forces—perhaps the most willing inductee of his day.

● ● ●

The spitball was once again officially outlawed from baseball in 1974, and maybe this time the prohibition will work. This was the third, and by far the most severe, edict directed at the unsanitary and extremely effective delivery, for it permits an umpire to call an instantaneous ball on any pitch that even looks like a spitter as it crosses the plate. No evidence is required; no appeal by the pitcher to higher powers is permissible. A subsequent spitball or imitation thereof results in the expulsion of the pitcher from the premises, *instanter,* and an ensuing fine. Harsh measures indeed, but surely sufficient, we may suppose, to keep this repellent and unfair practice out of baseball's shining mansion forever. Surely, and yet . . . Professional pitchers have an abiding fondness for any down-breaking delivery, legal or illegal, that will get the job done, and nothing, they tell me, does the job more effectively or more entertainingly than a dollop of saliva or slippery-elm juice, or a little bitty dab of lubricating jelly, applied to the pitching fingers. The ball, which is sent off half wet and half dry, like a dilatory schoolboy, hurries innocently toward the gate and its grim-faced guardians, and at the last second darts under the turnstile. Pitchers, moreover, have before them the inspiring recent example of Gaylord Perry, whose rumored but unverified Faginesque machinations with K-Y Jelly won him a Cy Young Award in 1972 and led inevitably to the demand for harsher methods of law enforcement. Rumor has similarly indicted other highly successful performers, like Don Drysdale, Whitey Ford, and Bill Singer. Preacher Roe, upon retiring from the Dodgers in 1954, after an extended useful tenure on the mound at Ebbets Field, published a splendidly unrepentant confession, in which he gave away a number of trade secrets. His favorite undryer, as I recall, was a full pack of Juicy Fruit gum, and he loaded up by straightening the bill of his cap between pitches and passing his fingers momentarily in front of his face—now also illegal, alas.

It may be perceived that my sympathies, which lately seemed to lie so rightly on the side of the poor overmatched hitters, have unaccountably swung the other way. I admit this indefensible lapse simply because I find the spitter so enjoyable for its deviousness and skulking disrespect. I don't suppose we should again make it a fully legal pitch (it was first placed outside the pale in 1920), but I would enjoy a return to the era when the spitter was treated simply as a misdemeanor and we could all laugh ourselves silly at the sight of a large, outraged umpire suddenly calling in a suspected wetback for inspection (and the pitcher, of course, *rolling* the ball to him across the grass) and then glaring impotently out at the innocent ("Who—*me?*") perpetrator on the mound. Baseball is a hard, rules-dominated game, and it should have more room in it for a little cheerful cheating.

● ● ●

All these speculations, and we have not yet taken the ball out of the hands of its first friend, the pitcher. And yet there is always something more. We might suddenly realize, for instance, that baseball is the only team sport in which the scoring is not done with the ball. In hockey, football, soccer, basketball, lacrosse, and the rest of them, the ball or its equivalent actually scores or is responsible for the points that determine the winner. In baseball, the score is made by the base runner—by the man down there, just crossing the plate—while the ball, in most cases, is a long way off, doing something quite different. It's a strange business, this unique double life going on in front of us, and it tells us a lot about this unique game. A few years ago, there was a suddenly popular thesis put forward in some sports columns and light-heavyweight editorial pages which proposed that the immense recent popularity of professional football could be explained by the fact that the computer-like complexity of its plays, the clotted and anonymous masses of its players, and the intense violence of its action constituted a perfect Sunday parable of contemporary urban society. It is a pretty argument, and perhaps even true, especially since it is hard not to notice that so many professional football games, in spite of their noise and chaos, are deadeningly repetitive, predictable, and banal. I prefer the emotions and suggestions to be found in the other sport. I don't think anyone can watch many baseball games without becoming aware of the fact that the ball, for all its immense energy and un-predictability, very rarely escapes the control of the players. It is released again and again—pitched and caught, struck along the ground or sent high in the air—but almost always, almost instantly, it is recaptured and returned to control and safety and harmlessness. Nothing is altered, nothing has been allowed to happen. This orderliness and constraint are among the prime attractions of the sport; a handful of men, we discover, can police a great green country, forestalling unimaginable disasters. A slovenly, error-filled game can sometimes be exciting, but it never seems serious, and is thus never truly satisfying, for the metaphor of safety—of danger subdued by skill and courage—has been lost. Too much civilization, however, is deadly—in this game, a deadly bore. A deeper need is stifled. The ball looks impetuous and dangerous, but we perceive that in fact it lives in a slow, guarded world of order, vigilance, and rules. Nothing can ever happen here. And then once again the ball is pitched—sent on its quick, planned errand. The bat flashes, there is a new, louder sound, and suddenly we see the ball streaking wild through the air and then bounding along distant and untouched in the sweet green grass. We leap up, thousands of us, and shout for its joyful flight—free, set free, free at last.

Roger Angell is a writer and fiction editor for the *New Yorker*. His baseball books include *The Summer Game, Late Innings, Season Ticket, Once More Around the Park, Game Time,* and *Five Seasons: A Baseball Companion.* His most recent book is *Let Me Finish,* a collection of essays.

LEE GUTKIND is the founding editor of *Creative Nonfiction* and prize-winning author or editor of more than a dozen books, including *The Best Seat in Baseball, But You Have to Stand!: The Game as Umpires See It.* ANDREW BLAUNER is a literary agent in New York City and editor of *Coach: 25 Writers Reflect on People Who Made a Difference.*